"If you're a woman in business you need this book in your life. Having run events, podcasts and more with Suz, I know that her energy, experience, knowledge, boldness and ability to help women play big is contagious, I can't get enough of this woman. Congrats on an incredible book Suz!"

ERIKA CRAMER – @TheQueenofConfidence

"Suz has a knack for bringing awesome people together and creating memorable brand experiences. She's the go-to person when it comes to getting out of your comfort zone, playing bigger and building a stand-out and bold brand, so I'm thrilled to see her share her knowledge and tips through this book! How exciting."

JESS RUHFUS – Founder of Collabosaurus

"Suz is a deadset LEGEND. If you want to step out confidently in the world but you're not sure where to start (or just sometimes get a bit wobbly) – this lady has your back. She combines the smarts of Sansa with the guts of Arya (and a wardrobe that leaves Daenerys for dead) and ensures everyone who connects with her unlocks the big, bold brilliance they have within. Your new empire starts here."

JADE WARNE – Founder of Hipster Mum, Photographer & Digital Marketer

Play Big, Brand Bold

Play Big, Brand Bold

IT'S YOUR TIME TO STEP UP,
SHOW UP AND STAND OUT!

SUZANNE CHADWICK

CONTENTS

—

ACKNOWLEDGEMENTS

N one of us are an island and I know that over the years there have been so many people who have helped me along the way. I think it's always important to reflect on the relationships you've had and the people that helped you get to where you are today, the ones who inspired and challenged you.

To Gareth – Thanks for hanging in there, loving me and being the support I needed to achieve the things I really wanted to along the journey, even when the risk was big, the crazy was real, and the outcome was never guaranteed. Whilst I've been at home and travelling to chase my big dreams you've held down the fort. You are an incredible dad and an amazing example of a strong and caring man in our home and I love you.

To Mum and Dad – You've taught me to be bold, supported me to dream big and loved me unconditionally, and that has made all the difference. Watching you both do big things, stay strong in your faith, have unwavering belief and speak up has always been inspiring to watch – so thanks!

To Sian and Ethan – Know that anything is possible. You have what it takes to live an extraordinary life, my amazing, strong, brave, and unique children. You are enough, and I will always believe in you and what you're truly capable of.

To my work friends, colleagues and leaders, thanks for giving me amazing opportunities to grow into the leader I always wanted to be. Thanks for listening, backing me and saying yes when I asked for so many different things. Your friendship and support has meant the world and you've helped me achieve so much, and still do.

WE RARELY
FAIL BECAUSE
WE DON'T
KNOW WHAT TO
DO; USUALLY
IT'S BECAUSE
WE'RE NOT
WILLING TO GET
UNCOMFORTABLE
AND DO WHAT IT
TAKES.

INTRODUCTION

—

The more I work with clients, speak at events and train teams, the more I think this is so true in the kindest way. I think so many of us want big things for our lives. I'm sure you do. And I know I do. The truth is that we have access to endless information on how to do a lot of the things we want, but there are visible and invisible things that stand in our way. I learnt early in my career managing large corporate teams and then later in life when I started working with business owners that what we want to do and what we think we're capable of or willing to do are two very different things.

What I know for sure – and as I sit here at 5.39am writing, it's literally staring me in the face stuck to my multi-coloured Kikki K yearly white board planner, is a quote that says – 'Anything is possible if you're brave enough Suz'.

If you've got this book in your hot little hands, then I'm guessing you want to do big things. Saying that – big can look any way you like. What seems big to one person may be small fries to someone else. So, before we get started on our journey together, let me just premise my message with this. You do you.

But hopefully it's a bigger, bolder version of you, and yes that can look any way you want it to.

So, you want to stand out, play bigger and you're ready to step up! Fantastic.

Well, of course you are – you're here, aren't you? So, I'm here to help and inspire you to make that happen. Do you know why? Because I made a choice a few years ago that every day I would wake up and say – today I'm choosing to show up. I'm choosing to do what it takes, hard or easy, or go down in flames trying. But at no point will I settle for average, boring or mediocre in life or business. Then I get my coffee, turn on some tunes, do my thing and tomorrow I get up and I do it all again.

Don't get me wrong, I don't always feel like it, but as I've learnt and I hope you'll learn too, the thoughts that start your day, rule your day.

Now before we dive in, I just want to tell you something. Anything is possible! I know that sounds totally cliché, but I started this book years before I finished it. Not because I've been toiling over it, perfecting my craft and honing my creativity, but because I could not make my damn mind up. I thought I would write a book, and then decided I wouldn't, then I would, then I couldn't, why bother, what's the point, blah, blah, blah – you get the idea.

Then something happened – well, someone happened actually. After listening to *Big Magic* by Elizabeth Gilbert (if you haven't read it, run out and get it immediately – well, after you've finished reading this book obviously) for the umpteenth time, she said, and I'm paraphrasing – "get your work out there. It doesn't have to be perfect and it doesn't have to be a masterpiece, but if you don't put it out there then you've wasted an opportunity." Thanks Liz, you are my creative cheerleader for life.

So, before we even get started, I just want to say off the bat, if there is something you've been wanting to do but have been putting off, if there is something you think could be fun or hard or exciting that you think is worth doing, then start today. Who knows where it'll lead – it may not lead anywhere, but at least you did it, and you can stop wondering what it would have been like if you were brave enough to take action. Now is the time to stop procrastinating and start playing bigger by choosing to show up and do the things that aren't always easy like branding bolder, but by the end of this book I really want you to learn how to love what you're putting out into the world, and that means learning how to build a *confidently bold brand*!

Okay, enough of my yammering, let's get on with it, shall we?

Hi, my name is Suzanne Chadwick but you can call me Suz. I'm like one of those persistent and inquisitive 6-year-old little boys (I know, I have one!) who asks a million questions about everything in life, love, the universe and I'll ask a million questions about you too! You can ask my husband – dating me was fun for his introverted self, but obviously he couldn't help but fall in love with me and my never-ending stream of questions. C'est la vie.

When you've been asking questions for 20 years, you learn a lot. You not only learn a lot, but asking questions becomes a way of life, and then if you're smart, it becomes a way of business. When you live in a time when you can ask Google anything and information is at our fingertips, nothing beats asking a question to a living, breathing person and getting an answer that is thoughtful or that has been realised through experience. Saying that, my husband has it down to a fine art when it comes to answering questions he doesn't know the answer to and can do so with full confidence, which leaves you wondering if he's actually right or not. Very sneaky and slightly unsettling.

This book is about asking questions, or to be more specific, asking yourself and others the right questions. Questions that get you the answers you're looking for. Questions that provide unique insights so you can keep learning along the way – whether you're learning a new skill, a new way of thinking or you want to find out more about your target audience to grow your business and brand. It's about being in a constant state of exploration, so you stand out from the crowd in a way that is uniquely your own.

It was September 2008, and we had just arrived back to Melbourne after I had lived in London for eight years. We had been home for three months. I felt starved of amazing, creative, female conversation and connection, and I felt like I was drowning sitting in my little two-bedroom rental unit in

Carnegie with its beige carpet and white walls. How had I gone from the vibrancy of London with all my friends, amazing bars and restaurants, and a challenging and incredible professional career managing a large recruitment team for a big four consulting firm to sitting on a beige carpet in Carnegie completely directionless?

I had been looking for a job, and there was nothing out there. So, not only did I not have any friends because they were all back in London and my old Melbourne friends had moved on after eight years, but I didn't even have a job to go to. As an extrovert, being alone is an unfamiliar feeling and reality to be faced with in a place I thought was home, and it was excruciating.

Coming home wasn't as easy as I thought it would be; after all, I was coming "home", right? I was bringing my new shiny Welsh husband back to the place I loved, and I thought it would be a breeze. It would be fun, we'd settle straight back in and life would be wonderful and effortless. It couldn't be this hard coming back.

Wrong. I struggled – like seriously struggled. We both did. I had met one or two women who I seemed to connect with, but after being surrounded by a large number of incredible ladies in London I thought – is this it? Where are the great women who I can have interesting conversations with? And like a lost singleton – where the heck do I go to find them? When you're in your 30s, how do you start all over again making friends? I felt like I was back on the 'dating' scene, and it wasn't looking good. After a few months, I found myself a new job in the boondocks in Port Melbourne working onsite for a large pharmaceutical client amongst the factories. I know – glamorous, right?

I had a brainwave – I wanted to start a business where I would buy discontinued designer clothing at a bargain price online and then run catwalk events where people could come along and purchase said garments straight off the catwalk whilst they sipped their fabulous cocktail, laughed, and spent loads of money darling, darling. The idea made me giddy. Who wouldn't love that?

So, I ran a little focus group with friends over a glass of champagne (I was starting the brand experience early), I started buying, buying, buying, and I started exploring venue options. This went on for a few months, but it never got off the ground because, of course, women want to try things on and just because you have the measurements of a garment doesn't mean it looks good on you. Also, who wants to try dresses on in a dark bar with a drink in hand? Idea one not quite there, Suz. So, I sold the clothes on eBay and got rid of the rest. Yes, if you live in Oakleigh you may find a Marc Jacobs jacket at the local St Vinnes with the price tag still on it! Lucky you! Strike one. Hmmm now what?

What I hadn't realised is that I had been bitten. Do you know what I'm talking about? It's the day you had a realisation you wanted more, something bigger, something that was your own? Do you remember that day? Have you had that day? If you have, I can guarantee that you'll know the day I'm talking about and maybe even the moment I'm talking about. Now, things don't always run smoothly, and you may take different turns here and there along the road I like to call the business journey once you've been bitten. All you know is that you're on the hunt, the hunt for that big idea, that one thing you know you want to do more than anything else, and I was hot on the trail of my idea as it wove its way through several iterations and took me on my own little business journey. But more on that later.

Jump forward to 2013 and I had attended a number of business events and networking groups and called myself the goldilocks of networking. They were too big or too small or not conveniently located to home or they just weren't 'my peeps'. I would stand alone in rooms that felt cliquey with my glass in hand, moving in and out of conversations that left me feeling, well, blah. I was always amazed that I would walk into a room and the host would just leave me standing there on my own.

Come on people – seriously!!

So, as they say, if you can't find what you're looking for then it's time to create it yourself.

So, the question was – what was the most important thing for building this community? I had seriously never intentionally gone out to create a community before; it had just kind of happened in the past. The most important thing – connection. Feeling connected personally, professionally, being able to have a laugh but know 100% that you're not the smartest person in the room is so important. A place where I can have fun, learn, grow and connect with others. There were a lot of iterations of what I thought it could look like.

So, what to call the business… Empowered by Connection, Connect and Empowered, embrace, empower, shine, radiate, Build to Beam, wow really? There were definitely some average ones in there! But eventually with the brain dump, thesaurus trawling and feeling into all the words – The Connection Exchange came through. The minute I wrote it down, I knew that was it, and as soon as I registered it, I trademarked it too. In for a penny, in for a pound!

When you know you know!

So, in March 2014, I excitedly registered my business The Connection Exchange.

It's amazing when you find 'the one' – yes, it was thunderbolts for me when I met my hubby on that rainy, cold night in London at the Grays Inn Road Pub speed dating (true story), and it's kinda the same when you find your business name and it hits you! Well, maybe not as life changing as finding your life partner, but you know what I mean! So, off I went. How hard could it be really to start a business? That is the question isn't it?

What is this book about I hear you ask? It's about my journey, but mostly it's about sharing how you can play bigger, learn to build a brand with soul that you love and your customers love even more, and it's about helping you to stand out in the sea of sameness. It's about the lessons I've learnt along the way asking hundreds if not thousands of questions and how branding bold took my business from small biscuits to delectable and awesome Tim Tam goodness.

the

JOURNEY

—

ONCE A CORPORATE CHICK, ALWAYS A CORPORATE CHICK

Chapter One

—

LONDON CALLING

I thought I would always be somebody who worked in corporate and climbed the corporate ladder to be bigger, better, earn more money, and manage bigger teams and even bigger projects. It was really the only thing I was planning on doing, and I won't lie – I was and still am an ambition cat. I find it really interesting that this is where I ended up. Working from home in Melbourne, working day in and day out with amazing women in business, plus working with global multinational organisations to deliver their employer branding projects. It's a pretty exciting place to be, but it's really not where I ever imagined or pictured myself. Growing up in Melbourne, to what I thought was a pretty middle-class home, I was fortunate enough to have parents that always looked at giving us, my sister and I, the best chance when it came to our life and education.

I was born in South Africa in 1976. My parents had lived through the apartheid system, and with my mother classified as 'coloured' and my dad being fair, was assumed to be 'white', there were some pretty interesting and, what I always thought, sad stories they shared with us. One night my parents were travelling with my sister and I. We stopped at a motel for the night, and my dad went in to book the room. The person behind the desk said yes, not a problem, there was a room available. When my dad went to get my mum, my sister and I, the same person said they had no rooms left. It's just not something I can even imagine going through, and it broke my heart to hear that my mum had to experience that.

When I was barely two, my parents migrated to Melbourne, Australia with $50 in their pocket. When we arrived in Melbourne, we lived with my grandparents in a little two-bedroom unit in Camberwell. Yes, that's right, six people in a two-bedroom unit – cosy. My mum and dad worked and always gave us a happy home, which is what I remember. That and the swearing cockatoo my grandpa owned who would greet you at breakfast time with a very loving "good morning darling" – the cockatoo that is, not my grandpa.

Once we moved into our own unit, I remember sprinklers in the front yard and icy poles during hot summers. I remember our labrador, Nikki, running around, tearing holes and eating the corners of the couch. I remember playing with the neighbours and riding our bikes up and down the three-unit driveway; a pretty typical Melbourne upbringing. My dad had had his own business in South Africa but was now working in a factory in Melbourne as a supervisor. Whilst he was still in a job, he started up Garcian Doors on the side. He eventually left his job and went into his own business full-time, which he still runs today.

We moved again when I was seven, then years later after being at the local high school for three years and not doing well – because it wasn't cool to do well – my parents sent me to a private school in Melbourne, where I successfully sat for a scholarship.

I joined Kilvington Girls' Grammar (now co-ed) in year 10, at 15 years of age, which is never an easy thing to do, but I was fortunate to find a group of girls who I still keep in contact with today, who were always fun, supportive, and great to be around.

Once I was in an environment where doing well, studying and trying to be the best in the class was expected and encouraged, I thrived. Even then I was competitive and ambitious; I knew that I always wanted to do bigger things. In year 10, I joined the school debate team and found something that I truly loved. The adrenaline, excitement, nerves and competition were amazing. We would compete with other schools and even debated at state level. That's where I found my love for public speaking and never looked back! The rush of being on stage, having all of those eyes on me and passionately trying to convince the audience in front of me that of course public transport should be free! Getting up, calmly walking centre stage and starting off: Madam Chair, ladies and gentlemen – today we're not just talking about whether public transport should be free. We're talking about the type of society we want to live in… and off I would go, guns blazing with rebuttal arguments, pauses and inflections at just the right time and my Italian hand movements flying through the air. It really was fun!

Even though I went to university, I also got a job straightaway working in a telemarketing company. I wanted to be working and earning money. So, I moved out of home at 19 with a work friend, who was a New Yorker, to Toorak.

Now for those who are not from Melbourne – Toorak is the most expensive suburb in Melbourne and no, I didn't choose it, my lovely new flatmate Steph – said New Yorker – came into the office and informed me we would be living in Mathura Road right in the heart of Toorak Village. So, with my $24,000 salary I had about $600 left a month after rent. Lucky we knew all the cheap pubs and had an endless supply of two minute noodles! We borrowed furniture from friends and danced in the living room a lot. They were pretty amazing days.

After working awhile, at the ripe old age of 19, I became the administration manager. I kept studying for my marketing degree at Swinburne University and then went and temped at a recruitment company and quickly secured a full-time job there.

At 22, I was working in Melbourne as a senior consultant. I loved my job, to say the least. I was young and working as an IT recruiter in the Y2K era – that meant big business, big money and lots of partying (in a nutshell). I had no particular direction, but I knew that I was living a good life and that was good enough for me. When you can buy a new car outright with a single quarter's bonus of $20k, you know you're doing okay.

That year my CEO offered to transfer me to the London office, and like any normal 22-year-old I said YES YES YES – what did I need to think about? An adventure had been handed to me, and I was ready – oh so ready to spread my wings and see where it took me. As soon as the offer was made, I was on a plane to London via New York City, where I visited my old Melbourne flatmate, Steph, for a full month along the way.

Now, with my time in London, there is a lot I could share with you… it could be a book in itself from crazy last minute weekends in Paris to dancing in a tiny Farringdon club with Boy George on the decks and leading the charge of 40 or 50 party revellers in tow through the streets of Barcelona during my hens weekend as we nightclub hopped – but anyway, I digress.

Move forward four years, and I was working for a company who was contracted to one of the big four consulting firms in London. I was now managing the recruitment team, working stupid hours in a job I loved more than life itself and working with people who blew my mind. They were smart, fun, focused and challenging, and I thrived. I excelled in this environment, and here I learnt about strategy. The strategy of business. It was like someone had just handed me a map with clear parameters to achieving awesome things.

Now, remember that I was 25/26 at the time and had never worked in a business. When you're a recruiter, you're working to find people; you're not building things yourself, so it's far more transactional. In this new land I was expected to create campaigns, strategies, measure activity, forecast numbers and deliver outcomes to some pretty tough clients. But the more I did it, the more I loved it. I could predict my outcomes – how amazing is that? It was around 2005/2006 and LinkedIn had just hit, Facebook was gaining traction in the London market and I had discovered Twitter. We had used none of this for business as yet, but we were starting to. It was great creating new and innovative ways to attract and engage high calibre talent in the market through new branding messages, events and activities, and I had the spreadsheets and metrics to show how we were tracking.

From that moment on, if I was delivering anything, I was creating a strategy to make it happen. It made me feel in control, meant that we set milestones in place so we knew what should be happening and when, and then we celebrated when we achieved them. If we didn't achieve them, then we could go back and look at the metric and why we hadn't hit our numbers or achieved what we set out to achieve. The clarity of being able to do that is one of the most satisfying things ever because it's not personal; you have the data, facts and figures to explain the story you were telling yourself.

Now you might be saying, well Suzanne, there isn't much soul in that statement if it's not personal. What I want to convey and share in this book is that your business idea, the way you connect with people, your brand values and personality can be truly soulful and inspired, but the way you run your business must be hard core action, measurement, goals and understanding of what is going on.

So, over the next couple of years in that job, I worked my butt off from 6:30 in the morning to 11:30 at night. Partied the night away in London bars and clubs and would come to work and do it all again. I loved it, thrived on it and thought, *this is the life.* It was amazing. Travelling, friends, great jobs, great companies. I felt like I had found my place. It was super high pressure, long hours, surrounded by super intelligent and challenging people, and for a long time I thought – this is where I want to be, and this is where I want to climb the ladder.

Then one random evening a girlfriend asked me to be her wingwoman on a speed dating night (don't judge, it was all the rage at the time) at the Grays Inn Road Pub in Holborn, everything changed. As I sat across the table from 15 different men that evening, having four-minute dates, I met my Welsh husband. I don't know if you know 'the look' – the look someone gives you in an unexpected moment that sends the thunderbolt and lighting through your whole body. You know – that look. Yeah, I got one of those.

Fast forward two years and about 20 countries of holiday fun, including a working stint in New York, we were fortunate enough to get married in Thailand. On Koh Samui, my favourite place in the world. Knowing that the UK was never somewhere I wanted to settle down – mainly because of the weather – I knew I would always go home to Melbourne. I did tell my then-boyfriend on our second date that if he always wanted to live in the UK, then there was probably no point continuing to date. To which he said – sure I'd move to Australia. I'm not sure if he meant it at the time or as he's told me since, "I would have said yes to anything at that stage" – and so we moved back to Melbourne in 2008.

I knew that if we settled down, Melbourne was where I wanted to be. But it took a lot longer than I ever imagined it would to settle back in. I still joke that I'm sure it'll happen any day now. It's been 10 years!

Being in London taught me to be independent, ask for what I wanted, take risks, work hard and make the right alignments to achieve my goals. Besides it being a pretty amazing ride, little did I know that these lessons I had learnt would carry through to a business I hadn't yet created.

"IF YOU DON'T ASK, YOU DON'T GET"

Chapter Two

JUST ASK

n 2010, I was pregnant with my first child and working for an energy company managing a large recruitment team. It was okay, but I was getting bored and after being in the recruitment game for 15-odd years, I knew it was time to change things up. Then, late one afternoon in October 2010, 37 weeks pregnant, I sat on the 32nd floor of a large skyscraper in the city in a corner office with my client and a branding and social media consultant named Sam, a meeting that would change everything.

Sam had been brought in to support our recruitment efforts and was talking about how we'd use social media and branding to attract key talent in the market. This wasn't new to me, but at that moment, just as I was about to go on maternity leave, I knew I was done with operational recruitment and this was exactly what I had been looking for. As she sat there talking about the different things she could do, like building communities and audiences, engaging them with content and attraction strategies and campaigns, I was getting more and more excited because a light bulb had just gone off. This was what I had been looking for.

Now, at 37 weeks pregnant I wasn't really in a position to do much about this newly discovered exciting lightning bolt moment. So, four months after having my daughter, I contacted Sam on LinkedIn and offered to work for her a few hours a week free, if she taught me what she knew.

One thing I want to point out here – asking for what you want is how you get what you want.

People will say yes and people will say no and it doesn't really matter. When one door closes another will open, or you'll build a window and get in, or find another way. So, at the end of the day I had nothing to lose by asking. Had she said no, I would have worked something else out. I find that once an idea plants itself, like a seed, it's hard to stop it growing, and my seed had been planted without a doubt.

Over the next 24 months, I did everything in my power to learn all I could around branding, social media and marketing. I also had another baby along the way. From working with Sam to investing in a range of big and small online courses, I had discovered this new world, and I threw myself wholeheartedly into learning all I could about business, brand, marketing and everything in between. It was like a new fire had been lit, and I was ready to come out all guns blazing.

We worked together on different campaigns, building Twitter followings, looking at brand strategies, talking about what she was doing with clients. It was such an exciting time. I remember diving into that with a passion I hadn't had for a long time – probably since coming back to Australia.

At the same time, I started sewing – I know, totally random but that bug was still biting! I couldn't find any funky baby wear, so I decided to make my own. Little did I understand that the cost of buying material retail (hello Spotlight), the time it took me to actually make things, and the price I could sell it at, would never be profitable. But it was something I wanted to try and really enjoyed. I called it Stylise, and I'd go to markets on the weekends and sell my goods.

I would also sell on Etsy and madeit.com and put all of my sewing wears out there. They started to sell, and the one thing I loved and hadn't really experienced before was customer engagement and conversation. I loved the comments from customers and the community. I'd have women saying – "I love these fabrics, they are so bright". Or someone would come along and say, "My friend told me to find you!" Ummm, how amazing is that?

Having worked in the corporate sector for so long it felt so different to create a physical product myself and have people love what I made. Even though I didn't make a million dollars, it did okay, and I knew that working with my own customer base was something I definitely wanted more of.

Whilst moonlighting doing social media consulting support and branding and then having my little Stylise sewing business whilst still on maternity leave, I knew deep down it was time for a change and the corporate job just would not cut it on its own anymore.

When I finally returned to work after two back-to-back maternity leave stints, it was time to have a few key work conversations. I had conversations with one or two of the leaders in the business I was in and shared that I was ready for my next move. One thing that I've learnt throughout my career is to be open and honest with the people with the power to make things happen in your world. When you're younger it's your parents, when you start work it's your bosses and when it's your own business it's the decision makers who may be solo clients or it may be companies you want to work with. These conversations require two key things. One is the ability to build solid relationships and the second is the courage to ask for the sale, or for what you want.

A job swap opportunity was quickly put on the table with my recruitment lead role and an employer brand consulting role in the business. I couldn't believe my luck – this was exactly what I had wanted. It was only because I had shared what I really wanted that the opportunity came my way, because all the conversations had happened behind closed doors.

Beyond excited about diving into my new role, I started planning out what I would do in this role. We had been doing projects here and there for clients but hadn't formalised the pricing, packaging and delivery. I developed a proposal for my CEO on how we could charge for the services we provided, and I put all the training and newfound knowledge I had gained over the two previous years whilst on maternity leave into action.

As I built out the structure of the consulting offerings, I immersed myself in working on the project methodology, pricing and packaging, frameworks, messaging and more.

In 2013, a girlfriend who had been in an amazing corporate role had just had a baby and decided that she didn't want to go back. Not even realising the skills I had been developing and what I'd learnt over the last year or two, she said, "Sue, how did you put together your pricing and packaging? How did you build that project methodology? How did you go to market with all these things?"

I walked her through the steps I had taken. I had no idea I actually had the knowledge or the skills to teach somebody else – that's where it all started. She was the first of a number of friends I supported and helped, and then women I worked with who were asking me business questions here and there.

It's amazing what you learn along the way! Sometimes you may not know how much you know until you help someone else do the same. Over time I worked with a few friends to develop their brand strategy, marketing, pricing, and packaging and had that second wind of excitement. Helping others do what I had done was fun, interesting and felt 100% right. The more we worked together the more they would say, "Suz, you have to do this and get paid for it." I hadn't really thought about it, I was just having a great time supporting them planning their world domination over wine at dining and kitchen tables.

To learn more and grow my network in this new-found entrepreneurial space, I attended networking events and found them harder than I felt they needed to be. It was awkward, and people would be left standing on their own for long periods of time – which always surprised me. I knew I wanted to connect with other driven women who most likely had come from a corporate background and were now doing their own thing, where I could have inspiring and challenging conversations around building this business. As open as I was to meeting new people, I just couldn't find what I was looking for, so I decided to create what I wanted.

It was time to take another leap to create what I wanted in my life and business, and if I couldn't find the women I wanted to connect with then I would build something to attract them.

On 14th March 2014, I registered The Connection Exchange. The Connection Exchange just felt like the right business name for what I was looking to create and build. And through the wonderful word-of-mouth from friends, clients quickly started knocking on my door, and I would consult on an hourly basis, when I had the time working around my full-time job. It wasn't perfect but it was a start and I was back to thriving again!

I knew that another 'ask' was on the table. As the business got busier I knew I wanted to shift the hours I was working in my corporate job to give me more time to build the business – so one Wednesday afternoon as I stood on the 20th floor of a skyscraper in the city, waiting for a design agency to pitch to our client on a branding project I was managing, I said to my director, "Can I chat to you about something later?" She immediately asked what it was about. I had decided a few weeks earlier that I would ask to go part-time, and I had been sweating over asking, worried that the answer would be no, and – obviously – the clouds would fall out of the sky. I made it such a big deal in my mind.

So, when she asked what it was about, I said, "I'd like to go to four days a week."

Her immediate response was, "Which day do you not want to work?"

"Wednesday."

"Fine."

And that was that.

Moral of the story: things are never as bad as you think they will be. We build things up in our heads and nine times out of ten they're a non-event.

So, ask for what you want!

PLAYING

Big

—

"YOU WILL ONLY TAKE UP THE AMOUNT OF SPACE YOU BELIEVE YOU DESERVE IN THE WORLD."

— *Me*

Chapter Three

WHY WE PLAY SMALL

Wow, where do I begin with this one? Talk about opening a can of worms. The reasons are endless and they're different depending on who you speak to, where they've come from, what's important to them and what they want.

I'll be honest with you here. When I started in business and was working with women to help them bring more structure, strategies and systems to their business, I had no idea how big of an issue this was.

I'd always been an ambitious cat and so I assumed that when someone wanted something they just went after it – no? Yet the more I worked with women the more I saw them not doing what they had promised me and themselves they would do, or just coming up with excuses.

Apparently, they wanted this thing – this business. They wanted the dream of creating something that was important to them but for some reason, they weren't willing to do the work.

Why is that?

What was that?

I hadn't come across this in the corporate world. I'm not saying it's not there, it just wasn't something I had experienced to a great extent – or maybe I just hadn't noticed or wasn't aware of it. The stats show that a woman will only go for a job if she feels 100% qualified and a man will apply with only 70% of the skills needed. So, in this instance I was the man. I had always jumped in, put my hand up, said why not and then worked it out on the way there.

I remember standing in a large circle of my colleagues one afternoon back in 2007 as we had Friday night drinks and wrapped the week up. Tom, the Account Director at the time said, "We have a secondment opportunity in New York for four to six weeks if anyone is interested."

Before he could even finish the sentence, my hand was in the air.

Did I know who the client was? No.

Did I know where I would be living? No.

Did I know what was involved? No.

Nope to all the above. No idea – but I knew I wanted to live in New York for a month, and I knew I wanted someone else to pay for the privilege.

Sure, I was two months out from getting married – but really, did that matter? Hell no!

This is a once in a lifetime opportunity, and I wasn't about to let it pass me by!

So, two weeks later I was on Madison Avenue, snow melting on the sidewalk, a Starbucks in one hand and cream cheese bagel in the other, breathing in the fresh New York air as I walked the nine odd blocks to the Credit Suisse offices where I would be working for the next month. It was bliss! Another colleague, from Scotland, who I had never met before had also landed the gig. So, every night he and I would head out to a new restaurant, bar or club and see the sites. I caught up with my old Toorak flatmate, and my fiancé came over for a long weekend. Once again, I could write another book on all that, but I'll leave that for another day.

Shifting your mindset to one of action, seizing opportunities, looking for opportunities or creating opportunities will literally change your life and business. That is no exaggeration!

So, back to my clients. When I started my *Play Big, Brand Bold* journey I interviewed 50 women in business. They were very generous with their time, and sometimes we would be on the phone for over an hour as they answered all my (annoying six-year-old little boy) questions of "but why". There were some tears and some realisations as we talked about what holds them back, and it was one of the best things I did for my business and my own understanding of my clients. It helped me not only write this book but it helped me build my business to create a product that is now my signature course, Brand Builder's Academy.

I think it's always important to start out understanding what Playing Big actually means to people. The answers I got were varied and always interesting. Here are just a few.

"Playing a bigger game to me is very closely intertwined with success. I would define it as stepping out of my comfort zone and succeeding in areas that I wouldn't have been able to do before. Confidence is a big thing, everything comes back to that feeling – like we don't have the skills, we're not good enough, we don't know the small steps to get to the bigger steps. It's hard to break down in your own head if you're not getting the guidance. We don't spend the time to plan out how to get from A to B and we're doing all this other work on our business, work, families and so it always seems out of our reach."

"Playing Big is putting yourself out there in every way possible, being known, and having that presence, putting everything on the table."

"Playing Big means expansion, not fearing it, knowing I'm capable and have what it takes. It's the fear of – what if I make it – what if I can go bigger and bolder, which is scary. The fear of Success. I'm drawing a blank as to why that would be a bad thing. Is it something that I've been told but I don't know why? Maybe it's because I would be responsible for so many people's businesses. It means I may be responsible for their success. I'm putting pressure on myself for what their success looks like."

"Not just reaching your goals but doing as well as you perceive is possible within your niche or marketplace, being known and going above and beyond. Being invited to speak about what you're doing, being a role model, being seen as a leader in my area."

I spoke to one person who I knew was an introvert and works specifically with introverted business owners, so I wanted to also know what her definition of playing big was.

"When you're an extrovert you speak up, think quicker and act faster, usually. The world celebrates the go-getter, doer, extrovert and people who are not like that may not feel like they can dive in. Sometimes we need someone who can move us forward and bring us out of our shells. It's the notion that people are moving faster than me. I think the key is learning your own processes and working out how you work and think rather than trying to do what everyone else is doing. Know your message inside out."

Sometimes it's even the people who teach it that struggle with it. One person said:

"Visibility, it's very easy for me to teach people to do it but I find it very hard. I think about not being good enough, worried about people taking my ideas and copying them (which has happened). My monkey mind then says they are better than you anyway."

Another said Playing Big was:

"Being international, being well known, fully stepping into the realm of having a million-dollar business, being the main breadwinner. Like the people we know – Marie Forleo, Denise Duffield-Thomas, consistently showing up and being seen."

After talking to all these women about what Playing Big meant to them, one thing I wanted to know was when you're not Playing Big or doing the things you really want to do – what exactly are you doing? Self-awareness is one of the biggest assets you can have as a business owner, so this question was really important. Here were some of their answers:

"I'm really introverted so I choose to stay a lot. The weeks where I'm

playing big and doing the things I think I should be doing, I see all these other professionals and coaches playing big and putting themselves out there and sometimes I feel like I can't do that. I want to but I can't. I don't know how to be so bold or transparent. I see these people who share so much of their lives, and I'm a very private person so I really struggle with that. I struggle to find the line of how much to share."

"I procrastinate – not being productive in the right areas and just doing things that aren't going to get me where I need to be. Not having a structure or a strategy means I don't know exactly what I should be doing. I plan but then I don't do what's on my plan. Maybe I do this because I don't know what actions to take to get there. I know what I want to achieve but then I don't know how to break it down into smaller things."

"I know all the things I can do but I haven't done it. It's taking that shift of it being a hobby to really making it a business. I procrastinate with things I don't know how to do."

"I'm not a small person – I'm a size 24. I have a limiting belief that you have to look a certain way. It's the public persona as to how I should look. I want to create an online course but I have an issue with the video side of things and people will see me."

"If it's not perfect then I'm not doing it, basically. I know that holds me back most of the time but I don't really know how to change it."

"I'm still doing the things that I know I shouldn't be doing. I'm doing the things that I should outsource. I need to put boundaries around what I do."

"I feel like I do a bit of self-sabotage where I think – what if I actually do it? I feel like there is something where I pull back or don't play full out. Sometimes when I get the gig I think – what now? I also do the thing where I have an idea and I think – that will be great. And then I don't do it. Because I've been doing it on my own for so long, you start to feel like you're wading through molasses. My partner has recently come into my business and is doing more of the tech stuff which has been great."

Now you might be wandering why I included all these responses. The main reason is so you can hear all the different reasons. Maybe you identify with one or two or none of them. We all have our own things but being self-aware of what they are, what's holding us back and what we can do to shift ourselves is one of the most important messages I want you to get out of this book.

When I'm speaking to a group of people I always say, "If you take nothing else away from today, I want you to remember this…". So, I will say it to you – if you take nothing else away from this chapter I want you to remember that if you can't see what's holding you back, if you can't be self-aware and take action then you'll stay stuck for a very long time. My good friend Erika Cramer, The Queen of Confidence says, *"If you keep sweeping your shit under the rug, it's going to trip you up every day – so you have to deal with it!"*

After the interviews I conducted and from my time working with women in business over many years, I've narrowed it down to five mindset minefields that keep us playing small. Now there may be other mindset snags you get along the way, but a lot of it falls into these five key areas, and we will work through each one together.

MINDSET MINEFIELD #1
CARING WHAT PEOPLE THINK AND ASKING FOR PERMISSION

There are so many things that hold us back, but this, from my experience is the number one reason. What will they think? Whether it's your friends, family, partner or random strangers on the internet, for some reason we worry. We worry about what they'll think, what they'll say and who they'll say it to.

Before we dive into this deeper, there are two sayings that have saved me with this minefield. If you haven't guessed by now, I love my quotes.

The first one is: People will like you and others with loath you and it will have absolutely nothing to do with you. I pull it out fairly regularly especially when I speak with others who feel the need to listen to everyone around them. It means that if you just get on with what you're here to do then you will have fans and foes. People will love you because of your values, how you show up, what you have to say and how you say it really resonates with them. Other people will feel the exact opposite, and that's fine.

The second saying is: Nobody who has accomplished more than you will ever judge you. Isn't that awesome? Basically, if someone is having a go at you really look at whether they should be someone you should be listening to. I love this more than I can tell you.

Everyone has their own idea of what their life should be. We also have an idea of what we think other people's lives should be, too, which makes us judgemental, opinionated and sometimes cruel in our eagerness to make sense of why people are doing things we either wouldn't do or we're not brave enough to do.

If caring what people think and asking for permission is something that you struggle with, then a few things may have contributed to that. One is that it's kind of how we were brought up. We've been taught that we must ask permission to do things, and then we look for validation once it's done. So, when you're a kid you must ask your parents for permission to do that thing, and then we get graded for the work we do. We ask our friends if they like the guy we're dating, whether they like what we're wearing and all the rest of it. It's how we're conditioned. Do we fit in? Is what I'm doing right? Does this look right, do I sound right? So, let me just say – it's totally normal. Saying that – this is something you can 100% break, change and move away from in your life and business.

Five ways you can stop thinking about what people think:

1. Start trusting yourself – This is pretty big. When we start in business it can feel normal to poll everyone you know with the same question. Like, should I have my pricing on my website? What should my pricing be?

Should I post this on social? What should I wear? And the hundreds of other questions you ask. This is where you need to start trusting yourself.

Something I learnt to do early in my business when making decisions was this: I would try and understand two to three different opinions or actions I could take. I would assess them and decide which one felt right for me. I would act on it, and more. For example, when I asked myself, *should I have my pricing on my website?* There were a few options:

a. I could not have my prices on my website, which meant that people would need to contact me to find out what they were. This meant that I would sometimes speak to people whose budget didn't match what I charged.

b. I could have people download my pricing, which was gated. I experimented by opting in to find out pricing on someone else's website, but then when I received their pricing, it was about $10k out of my price range, and then I'm on a list of someone who I'm not an ideal client for.

c. Or I could just have my prices on my website – because that's what I like, because it helps me decide if this person is someone I can afford to work with.

Educate yourself on your options, work out what would work for you and your audience best, then decide. End of story. When you ask every woman and her dog, you'll just keep chasing your own tail!

2. Stop asking others for their opinions and seeking validation – everyone has their own filter of what 'good' looks like to them based on their experience and what they believe – which may not be what you believe or what you want. So, if you can trust yourself, then you can stop asking for other people's opinion and seeking their validation.

This might sound a little harsh, but we make decisions most of time based on what's best for us. So, seeking validation from someone with their own agenda means that their response may benefit them and not you. Remember, I may not encourage you do something that I'm scared to do myself.

The freedom you will feel when you stop looking for validation from others will change your life!

3. Surround yourself with a small group of people doing bigger things than you, who can support and help you to do big things yourself – Now, we are not islands and I get that! There will always be a small and trusted circle of people who you can ask support from. BUT – and yes, BUT is in capitals – these opinions are just additional information from people you respect that can help inform your decision, but don't let them decide for you.

4. Don't be afraid to fail and be okay with being unique and different – I also think that we ask for other people's opinions or we care what they think because we don't want to be too different. From the time we are in school we were taught to conform.

Don't stand out too much. Don't be too loud. Don't be too different – you want to fit in.

It's hard to shake 20 years or more of that, but that's what Playing Big and Branding Bold is about. It's about being different and trusting yourself, so you can brand bold and stand out from the crowd. That's what you want! We're told our whole lives to fit in, and I'm now giving you permission (if you need it) to stand out. To be bold. To be different! That's why you're here, isn't it?

5. Self-coaching and owning your decisions – Owning your decisions is about celebrating your success and learning from the things that didn't work out. When you trust your decisions, you'll be okay with whatever outcome you get because you made it and didn't rely on anyone else. If you want to stop caring what other people think then stop asking. They don't want the same things as you, so why would they give you the advice you need. Listen to yourself. Take time out from the noise so you can hear your own thoughts.

I've always been a bit of a self-coacher. Basically, it's where I'll get a whiteboard or sheet of paper, and I'll treat myself like a client. I'll ask myself all the questions I would ask a client. I'll brainstorm and then critique it and work out what 'good' looks like. The more you do it, the more comfortable you'll be with self-coaching and the better you'll get at it too!

MINDSET MINEFIELD #2
WILL IT WORK

I was recently sitting with one of my clients and she said, "I know my mindset is holding me back. I constantly think, *is this going to work? What if it doesn't work?* and that's what's holding me back."

I'm going to dive into how you can test the market out in Chapter 6 – Make it Happen, but I wanted to touch on it here because you have to remember (and I think I first heard this from Seth Godin, all about our monkey mind) that our brain will always try and keep us safe. It will always give us all the reasons why we shouldn't be doing something that is new to us – because that's the safer option.

So, when your mind says, *will this work?* You need to respond and say, *well I don't know, but why not give a try?* You have control over your own mind. Your thoughts are not fact, they are just thoughts. They are your subconscious keeping you safe. It's saying, *Hey there Sarah, don't go over there. That's a little out of your comfort zone. Why not stay here where it's nice and safe and warm and we know what's going on. That feels better doesn't it?*

This is where making the decision to play bigger comes from. It's a conscious choice that today I will show up. I will get uncomfortable. I will do something that is a little scary and that maybe I haven't done before, but you know something – I want to do this. I want to try this. I want to say I gave it a shot, and I want to make sure that I'm not letting these thoughts – that don't rule me – make my decisions.

I can honestly tell you that as I lay on the pillow the other night with my husband, I said to him, "I have the monkey mind going".

He asked me what that was, and I said, "It's when you do something big (I had just sent this book to the copyeditor), and your mind starts up with 'This is going to be rubbish. It's not going to be very good. Do you really want to do this? What if they buy it and they hate it? What if it's a total flop?'"

So as I said to him and I'll say to you, being conscious that it's going to happen and why it happens will change your life, how you show up and will determine the things you do in this life and in your business. Every time you have a thought like that, I want you practise saying, "Yes it's scary and I might fail but let's do it anyway – what if it's amazing?"

You, my dear, are in control – every, single, day!

The more you do it, the more fun it becomes and the less resistance you'll have – trust me, I do it every day!

MINDSET MINEFIELD #3
COMPARISONITIS

Whenever I talk to clients or other women in business, one of the biggest blocks to playing big or moving forward is looking at what other people are doing. When you're still trying to find your key message or clarity around what you're doing, it is normal to look at others doing the same thing, so you can see what their message is and how they're saying it.

The problem is that you end up with someone else's voice instead of your own and potentially something that not only sounds like them but looks like them too. You don't realise that the more you look at other people's work it subconsciously filters into what you do.

One of the biggest pieces of advice I give people is to get inspiration from other industries or types of businesses, so that you're not looking at someone who does the exact same thing as you. Nailing your core message or what you want to be known for can also help you gain clarity on what you want to say and how you want to say it. It'll obviously evolve over time but it's a good place to start. I look to a few different businesses outside of my industry for coaching and women in business groups. I love Frank Body's tone of voice, I'm totally a Gorman girl (clothing brand if you don't know it) and Sunnylife is a lifestyle brand I love.

When I started looking at business coaches, I was seeing a lot of the same. It's not to say it's bad or wrong, but it definitely wasn't me. There was a lot of 'heart centred', swirly watercolour logos and what I would call vanilla. I wanted to be the bubble gum or hokey-pokey of the business coaching world. I wanted to be colourful, stand-out, bold, creative, and – if I'm honest – a bit loud. One thing you'll learn in business is that not everyone is for you. So, standing out can sort the people you want to work with and the ones you don't, and that is what you should focus on.

I found the people I wanted to work with through having lots of conversations, then reflecting and nutting out what I believe and what I know is my truth. The more you have those conversations, the stronger your message will become, and you'll be able to hone and craft it, so it is perfect for you. I rarely compare myself to anyone these days, because I'm staying in my own lane and if someone chooses to work with me – awesome – and if they don't, then I wish them well and hope they find what they're looking for.

The other interesting thing on this topic is that you must be conscious of what and who you look at, because people will only let you see what they want, so thinking someone is perfect will never be the whole story! So, take everything with a grain of salt and don't believe everything you see.

One thing I want to make sure you don't do when it comes to looking around you is never let what someone else is doing stop you from doing what you want. If I had a dollar for the number of times someone has said, "Oh no I'm not going to do that because so-and-so already has a similar product," I would have least $20. I joke, but it's not that funny. I've said it before; I rarely follow other coaches or people who do what I do, because it's normal to have those thoughts if you see someone doing what you were planning to do.

It creeps in and it plants those nasty little seeds.

Well, she's doing it so you can't.

You should have been quicker.

Hers will probably be way better than yours.

What's the point?

Seriously you can avoid all of that if you stay in your own lane and just do your own thing.

My point? STOP LOOKING AT WHAT EVERYONE ELSE IS DOING!

MINDSET MINEFIELD #4
IMPOSTOR SYNDROME

Impostor syndrome is where you're just waiting for people to find out that you're not the real deal and let me tell you – I know people so experienced in what they do who suffer from this.

It's that inner voice that most of us have, or it pops up every now and again, that questions what you're doing. Is that really good enough, do you know what you're doing, do you have the experience to take that project on?

It's how we handle things that makes all the difference. Impostor syndrome can affect our ability to price and package well, step up and stand out. If we believe we're not good enough, we don't know enough or what we have to say isn't worthwhile then it's going to be hard to build your business with that in the back of your mind.

Impostor syndrome can be lessened if you speak to yourself the way a friend would. For example, if your inner voice is saying you're not good enough, then what would your best friend say to that? They would be cheering you on, 'You've got this, you can do it, you've done it before, don't doubt yourself.'

We need to start being our own cheerleader and shut down those negative thoughts, because those thoughts could mean you say NO to something really awesome because you have a false sense of capability or worth.

Working through your impostor syndrome can be a process. Whether you suffer from this or not, one thing worth doing every now and again to help you play bigger, year-on-year or more often, is to realise the journey you've been on, the skills you've learnt and where you are now.

Here are some questions to ask yourself:

1. Why did you start your business?

There must have been a reason. You saw a gap in the market, or you love what you do, and you thought, I can make a go of this. I could do this and earn money; I've got the skills and talent to make this happen. There must have been a level of confidence if you paid to register your business and get started – so we know it's there.

2. When did you start in this field?

Are you in a new field, or do you have 10 years' experience? Remember that I said there are people with 5–10–20 years of experience that still go through this. For me, when I did this exercise, even though I've been in HR and Recruitment for almost 20 years (so not all my experience is directly related to what I do now), I've mentored women in corporate to speak out, play big, and own their worth for most of that time. You don't have to answer this literally, meaning you may have been doing what you're doing for years even if it's not in the capacity you're doing it in today. Value and credit all the experience that has gotten you to this moment.

3. What work have you done and who have you worked with?

Think about the projects, the clients, all the hours that you've put in. It all counts.

4. What have clients or people who you've worked with said about you?

This is a big one. What results or outcomes have you gotten for your clients? What have they said? When you're feeling like what you do isn't enough or you're not enough, then go back to those words. I love my client testimonials, it reminds me of the people I've worked with, the result they have gotten and why I do what I do, and there is no shame in going back to these when you need to. We all have down days, but don't let it stop you from doing things you want or need to do.

5. What's been your proudest moment in business or your career?

Once again, connecting your emotions to achievements can help you push through when you falter or lose faith in yourself.

6. What have been your key learning leaps?

Think courses, aha moments, times when you owned your worth.

For me there have been courses that I've done that have helped me double my pricing, structure my business better, build my packages, create real momentum and they've helped me learn key lessons and skills to do the work I do. The reason I think it's good to look at these learning leaps is because sometimes we still see ourselves as that junior copywriter who still has a lot to learn. When you're near the top of your game, you know what you're doing and how to do it and you know a lot more than most people around you with your area of expertise.

So, don't underestimate yourself.

MINDSET MINEFIELD #5
PROTECT YOUR HEADSPACE

Recently a client asked me if it was okay if she stopped having coffee with people who did the same thing as her, as they just wanted to pick her brain and find out what she was up to. She felt uncomfortable about it and didn't really want to tell them what she was doing because she was working it out herself.

I said to her you must be responsible for what comes into your 'space'. This is your physical space, your online space and your headspace. It doesn't matter what anyone else thinks – it's up to you how you work best and what works for you. The minute something triggers you, look at what it is and try and work out why, and then if it doesn't serve you – get rid of it.

I don't hang out with other business coaches who do the same thing I do, I don't tell everyone what I'm doing who aren't my target audience, I don't watch what other women in business groups are doing – I just focus on my patch of grass. The reason I've actively avoided all of this is because I know it can trigger me. It could potentially stop me from doing something I really want to if I see someone else do it – so I just don't look!

When you're looking at other people, you're not focusing on your part of the world. You can get pulled into comparisonitis and it's a waste of your time.

**This is a big one that I want you to own
– you're responsible for your space.
Protect it, own it and surround yourself with
women doing big things and who want to see you succeed.**

When we allow ourselves to be in situations or environments where we will not get the best result, we're actually self-sabotaging – so we do things we know won't serve us and won't give us the result we want. Becoming aware of what those self-sabotaging behaviours are means we can avoid them. Sometimes these are unconscious behaviours, but if it's holding you back you have to nail it and get rid of it.

Ninety-five percent of women I spoke to knew they weren't doing the work that would help them get to where they want to be, and they know a lot of their procrastination habits already.

Every day, I think, *how can I play big today? What will I do to move myself forward? What's one thing, big or small.*

One thing I've started to do every morning, and you're welcome to use it, is say, "Today I'm choosing to show up." It sets me up that today might be uncomfortable and that I might have to make an effort to show up, show my face, say hi and be present.

It may only be for one to two minutes of the day but it's something I consciously do.

So, my question to you is: what do you need to do to start showing up more?

The first thing is, what do you think you're afraid of? For me, in the early days, I found it super easy to do Facebook Lives in my closed groups because I had a trusted audience, but I was more afraid to do it on my public Facebook business page. I also feared doing Instagram Lives. So, I set myself a challenge that over two weeks I would do as many Insta Lives as I could, and I would sit in the discomfort of that. I can tell you that by the second or third live, it didn't feel so hard anymore and wasn't such a big deal.

What are some things that you think you're afraid of? Some things may be fears, and others may be habits. If it's a habit, it could just be a lazy habit of not doing the things you should be doing; you're not actually afraid to do it, you just can't be bothered.

One of the biggest business, confidence and time killers is procrastination.

When I asked my 50-plus ladies what they are doing when they are not doing the things they know they should or want to be doing in their business, I got answers like:

"Anything else."

"The washing or cleaning the house."

"Watching TV or pottering around the house."

"Going shopping or having lots of coffees with other people who are also procrastinating."

We all suffer from it or deal with it and it's nothing new. I recently listened to a podcast with Dr Susan David who wrote the book *Emotional Agility*, and she talked about procrastination in such an interesting way. If we think of procrastination as a regulator of our emotions, there are different strategies we can use that are good and some that are not so good. For me,

I've found going for a walk or just taking some time out to take a break helps me get my head back in the game. I've also used some of the not so positive strategies she talks about, which are things like boredom eating or getting on social for way too long! Each one gives us a sense of comfort but some are helpful and some are harmful.

Dr David says that when we're in these times of procrastination we must bring our values front of mind, which I love.

Often, we say to ourselves that we 'have to' do this thing or get on with this task. Dr David calls them 'have to goals' which come from shame or obligation. So, it's important to look at and know why you want to do something that you're putting off.

If you feel like you 'have to' but you don't know why you have to or that 'have to' goal isn't really aligned with where you want to go, it's worthwhile working out what you want to do and knowing exactly why you're doing it. This can help you to splash in the puddle for a while and then get on with getting things done. I always find that if I plan my week and projects out then I have key tasks to do and it helps me avoid procrastination most of the time. For example, when I started to write this book, I had an idea of what I wanted it to be about but wasn't 100% certain. Once I got super clear on the idea, the reason for writing the book and who I was writing it for, the book flowed and the energy was back. I think you have to know and be connected to what you're doing to really power through it.

If it's just admin then you have to ask yourself, should I be doing this, or should I be outsourcing it and getting on with the things I want to be doing in my business? My point is to know why you're not doing the work. Figure out what's holding you back, ask yourself the deeper questions and then put a plan in place to move through it. If you need help, then find a buddy you can connect with where you can support each other.

Don't let procrastination be your Achilles heel – you've got this.

So, the big question is… what can you do to break the habits you have that aren't serving you?

"IN ORDER
TO BE
IRREPLACEABLE
ONE MUST
ALWAYS BE
DIFFERENT."

— *Coco Chanel*

Chapter Four

YOU ARE UNIQUE

Right now, we see passion in abundance; it's everywhere we look. There are amazing quotes, images, Facebook groups dedicated to heart-centred entrepreneurs and those 'living life out loud'.

What I don't see very often is clear, clever, insightful business strategy and brand positioning. Knowing what you want your business to do and what you want to be known for can change the game. So many business owners dive into their business with bucket loads of passion, ideas, enthusiasm but aren't sure what they are looking to achieve; they just know that they want to build 'something' that means they get to do what they love and make six figures in their first 12 months.

As I'm driving over the Bolte Bridge on a dreary Melbourne day heading to the airport, I keep mulling over the word 'unique'. Since starting The Connection Exchange, unique has been my mission. How to be different, how to stand out and how to go against the grain. How do we create unique brand experiences for ourselves and for our customers? It's the holy grail of business branding and whilst many start out wanting to be unique, the pressure and comparisonitis can sometimes be too strong; following the crowd with the hope of achieving someone else's success takes over. As the online world continues to explode and everything feels like it looks the same, being unique is the one thing that's worth striving for.

I've met some unique people in my time. People who make you feel a certain way; those who stand out from the crowd because they go against the grain; those who stand out because they're consistent and just keep showing up. Brands and people like Brené Brown, Lisa Messenger, Richard Branson, Denise Duffield-Thomas, Elizabeth Gilbert, Amy Porterfield, and Gorman, just to name a few, are all businesses, people and brands I have some kind of emotional connection to. That to me is brand power. I may not be able to explain it, but there is something there that draws me in. There is a sense of belonging and a feeling that they're 'my people'. It means that any time I read something of theirs, see a pic on Instagram, communicate or connect with any of them whether it's online or in real life, it's a positive experience.

But what makes someone unique? The more I think about it, the more I realise that it's nothing you 'try' and be, but rather it's when you do your thing, your own way, that the magic happens. After spending a whole day with Lisa Messenger at EPIC Summit 2015, I realised that she was like that girl in school who was a little crazy and off the wall, who just did things her own way. She had followed her intuition and a hunch and created something that now seems like such an obvious stroke of genius. After recently being gifted and reading Richard Branson's book *Finding my Virginity*, he seems like the most normal person in the world, but someone who is passionate and willing to take calculated risks when making big business decisions. He is such a fascinating person, and I loved reading his story.

There are more people and brands that we'll look at throughout this book that will show you the formulated and unformulated approaches that many take in the road to being unique, one of a kind, unlike any other!

What's the point of being unique when there are so many other people out there doing what you're planning on doing? In a world full of copycats, it's easy to take the easy way out and just duplicate what others who have gone before have done. It's less time-consuming, effort, hard work and thinking to do, so why not take the easy way out?

As I look at websites, blogs and businesses, there is a sameness that feels blah. So many look the same and act the same and everyone seems okay with that. There seems to be a comfort in conformity. Taking risks and just doing your own thing is something that people find hard. Because we're all learning from each other most of the time, listening to someone else's advice or podcast, we're doing what they've done before, and when you're in that learning phase, it's important to not just become a carbon copy of your favourite person.

Someone once said, "The biggest challenge in life is to be yourself in a world that is trying to make you like everyone else." There is the very famous TED talk by Sir Ken Robinson entitled 'How Schools Kill Creativity'. From the beginning of our lives we're taught to fit in, follow the norm, abide by the rules and think the same way. These are the things we've been taught are acceptable and this is the way the world works. We go to school, then university, get a job, get married, have kids, work for a good company that provides you with security and then that's it – that's the way it goes. Now, the 'dream' is being flipped on its head as young entrepreneurs from age 14 build their empires, blog, create and challenge the status quo. The other day I even posted an image on my Facebook page of Greta Thunberg, a 16-year-old girl on strike for the planet who was on the cover of *Time* magazine. The next generation is definitely not afraid to be seen and heard, and I think we can take a leaf out of their book.

When I was in primary school and half of high school, I just went with the crowd. When I changed high school, I found my voice and my own unique take on things thanks to a teacher, Mrs David – who was about four feet tall, if that – in her beautiful red sari. She used to stand there and say, *"Suzanne, make your point. Be direct. Be clear about what you want to say. You have to convince and connect with the audience. Take them on the journey.*

Bring them with you. Make them feel what you're saying" as she coached the debate team. I can still hear and see her, a miniature power pack and an incredible inspiration.

The question is, what is it that creates that unique feeling, business or brand? Is it someone's personality that makes them unique? Their take on life? What they desire? Or is it random?

The difficult thing about being unique is so many have come before us and many of us have grown up in similar environments, coming through the same school system and same school of thought. We don't even realise it when we create something similar to someone else, as singer Sam Smith discovered recently. His song 'Stay with Me' was said to be the same chorus as Tom Petty's 'Won't Back Down' which eventuated in Smith having to pay Petty 12.5% of royalties from the song. Smith, who is only 22 years old, claimed to have never heard the song before. Which may be very true. But does that mean that all thoughts are now just regurgitated information or creativity?

That would be sad if it were true. But luckily, I don't believe it for a second.

As we face new times with technology moving at a rapid pace, environment issues on the rise and worldwide issues of terror, there are opportunities for unique thoughts, debates, and ideas to come to the forefront.

FINDING YOUR OWN VOICE

I love it when I meet someone and the way they think and speak feels like a breath of fresh air. You know the type of people that I'm talking about. They have a way about them – they see things differently. As Eleanor Roosevelt said, "Great minds discuss ideas, average minds discuss events, small minds discuss people." When you get in a room with someone who wants to talk about ideas, the world becomes a different place. Creating new things, products, services, and ideas is such an exciting place to be. It allows you to think about things that others don't, expand how things work in the world and how they could look.

If I asked you: how do you see the world? Do you know? Do you see through others' eyes or do you have your own take on how things work? I've always said to my clients and community that you have the power and opportunity to become a thought leader, because your experiences, the way you were raised, your take on things will always be different to someone else's. You have a voice, and it is unique if you take the time to dig into what you think about things.

One of the biggest factors with business is your mindset. The more I connect with women in business, the more the message comes blaring through loud and clear – "back yourself, believe in yourself, know that you can, don't worry about what others say, do the work and take the chance."

The other woman in my life is my mum who taught me to ask for what I wanted in life. Thinking you can ask for anything you want creates a sense of – anything is possible. Why wouldn't I ask? If I ask, then they may say yes, and if they say no, then I'm in exactly the same position I am in now – so who cares? As I write these words, I realise that to this day, it's never occurred to me not to ask.

WE CREATE THE BRANCHES

I once listened to an interview with Todd Henry, an amazing writer and speaker on leadership. He was on *MarieTV* a while ago, and they were talking about finding your voice. Google both their names and 'finding your voice', and you'll be able to watch it. Todd shares a conversation he had with a DJ named DJ Z-Trip and his comparison of creativity to climbing a tree. Z-Trip is responsible for the mashup movement where he takes different genres of music and mixes them together. Todd once asked him how he found his voice as an artist. Z-Trip shares that as an artist we all have these influences when we're growing up, and that's the trunk of the tree. We stay close to these influences, and once we get a certain way up the trunk you have to decide which way you're going to go. Are you going to step out on a branch? Am I going to step away from the trunk and from my influencers and start to find my own voice? No matter what you do in life, we all reach this crossroad.

Z-Trip goes on to say that he wanted to step out on a branch and start to find his own style. Henry, thinking that he's being clever asks, "well what happens if you go too far out on the branch?", and Z-Trip says that most people aren't willing to follow you out on the branch. They may follow for a while, but if you have enough courage you'll most likely be one of the few, if not the only one, out there. Because the branch gets thin, most people aren't willing to risk it.

Henry goes on to ask, what if the branch breaks? Z-Trip says, that's the beauty, if the branch breaks then it forms a new trunk and people start following you, because you start to become the influence in their life.

I can't tell you how many chills that story gives me. I think I've watched the video a number of times, and like *Big Magic* I get something new from it every time I listen to it. It also helps me to visualise myself on that branch and how I'm stepping out, showing up and stepping up to play bigger as the influencer rather than the one influenced.

If you're looking to find your voice, think about where you are in your journey and what you're doing that is unique.

"WHETHER
YOU THINK
YOU CAN OR
YOU CAN'T,
YOU'RE RIGHT."

— *Henry Ford*

Chapter Five

———

MIND OVER MATTER

We've already talked about the mindset minefields and – yes, as business owners – there are a lot. Your mindset will determine your success.

When I started in business, I had a mindset block I didn't even know I had until I started putting my pricing together. As a corporate consultant, I charged out what most consultants charged out per day, and I didn't think twice about it. Once I started in my own business I thought about my prices in a completely different way. I've got all these skills where I help organisations look at their employer brand. We look at strategies, I build out channels for communication, and how they will reach their audience, etc. What I'm doing in my own business is helping small businesses, entrepreneurs, and solopreneurs, to do the same thing. The question is – if I'm taking the skills I use every day and charge X for, when I come into my own business, why would I reduce that by up to 50%? It's insane.

SOMETIMES YOU HAVE TO DIG
A LITTLE DEEPER

I explored this side of myself, and why I was discounting my rates so heavily when the skills I use were no different. Obviously, when you pay somebody for a service, you're paying them for their expertise, what you will learn, what you will gain from working with them. Really the price shouldn't be any different, but it took some time to work through that. I had heard of Denise Duffield-Thomas and knew a few women who had gone through her Money Bootcamp, so I did some exploring. I signed up for a few of her free audios, webinars, etc., and eventually, when she was about to double her price, I jumped on board. I got into Money Bootcamp, which brought a lot of awareness to me as far as taking a look at where my money blocks were, where they've come from, and how to actually work through them myself.

I worked through her course, looking at my earliest memories of money, how money was spoken about in my family, how I managed my own money, and the patterns I had. During my 20s I was very much just flying by the seat of my pants. I was living in London, earning a good salary – once again, in a consulting-type role – and was just spending it. Travelling, shopping, going out. When it got to payday, I might have had two hundred quid in the bank, and that would have been it. I had always lived like that. Fortunately, I married a man who was the complete opposite. He was a saver and very sensible with his money. So, I started changing my habits to be more conscious and learn good money habits.

The other thing I was looking at was decluttering and looking at how I managed my money. Once I started to track everything, was using a good accounting software, running profit and loss reports and creating solid money habits, things started to get better. The more I did that, the more I could see the money coming in. As they say, what you focus on expands. Having clear pricing and days in the business where you track money, send out invoices, chase up invoices and see how you're going against your financial goals can transform your cashflow and your money mindset.

GETTING IT SORTED

Making sure that I was on top of my money situation, what was happening in my business, being aware of what was coming in and what was going out was one of the next challenges. So many women I've worked with start tracking their money and what's financially happening in their business later than they should! They think, I'll just see how it goes, which is what I did in the beginning too. No separate business bank account, a huge amount of software subscriptions and money being drained out quickly. I quickly started to count every dollar, made sure invoices were paid and that I knew exactly how much my monthly expenses were.

When you're at the beginning of your business journey, it's easy to step into the mindset of scarcity. Is this going to be the last client I have? Should I keep working ALL the hours in case this is it? Moving from a mindset of scarcity to one of abundance has been an ongoing journey and one that I work on daily.

Money mantras I've learnt from others along the way:
- This is what a wealthy woman looks like (when you look in the mirror)
- There's plenty more where that came from (with money in general)
- What flows in, flows out and flows easily back in (knowing that money can be fluid and that's fine)

I think when you get to the point where you have transparency across your business it can make a huge difference. I get that money can be a very triggering area in business, and in life, for so many people, but there is a way to create ease around it if it's something you focus on.

THE THREE PS – POSITIVE, PATIENT AND PERSISTENT

I grew up with a mother who loves alliteration, so you may see that come through a little (or a lot). Your money mindset may be one hurdle to overcome and – depending upon if you're a man or a woman – it will take hold of you in different ways. With any mindset, these three Ps are key for any business owner to be highly aware of:

1) Staying positive

2) Being patient

3) Being persistent

Believing you can, being optimistic about the outcome and thinking about all the ways you can work through a problem can mean the difference between becoming paralysed by inaction and working through the issues you come up against. Knowing there is a way and that, as Marie Forleo says, everything is figureoutable is key to your business journey. Without a positive outlook, you may get to where you're going, but it will take you longer, be more painful and you will find yourself in the puddle or the hole for longer than you need to be, which – to be honest – is not a great place to be.

Staying positive can be a conscious decision. Surrounding yourself with positive people, positive vibes, being self-aware of your mood and your thoughts. I have quotes around me that I can see every day. If, like me, you're a visual person these can really impact how you show up. If you keep hearing something is not good enough then that's what you'll believe.

When it comes to playing bigger, your current commitments and where you are in life will always impact or influence how much you can do, what's possible and how much time you have. If you have a job or if you have kids or if you have other responsibilities, then the question is – what can you still be doing with the time you have that can take you to the next level?

I remember talking to a woman I did an interview with. She said, "I just don't have the time and I'm not in a position to play big right now as I have small kids."

My question to her was, "What would playing big look like at this point in your life?"

Playing big will look different at different times in your life and what you're able to do right now in your life may not always look like this. In a few years, you may have more time. In a few years, you'll have more knowledge and skills. I mean really, who knows where you'll be or what you'll be doing – so play big where you are so it works for you. Consciously make that decision, and don't let not having everything you need right now stop you from doing what is possible with what you do have!

Always remember, when you change your thoughts, you change your actions which change your outcomes.

"NEVER LET
NOT HAVING
A CLUE
HOW TO DO
SOMETHING
STOP YOU!"

Chapter Six

—

MAKE IT HAPPEN

t's late October 2014 and as I continue to feel my way through growing The Connection Exchange, an idea hit. I'd seen so many different conferences around Melbourne, but none that had really grabbed me. I'm a woman in early stage business, and I want practical and actionable content I can use in my business straightaway. I want to be in beautiful surrounds with amazing women and I'm willing to pay for it. I'm not looking for cheap and cheerful – I'm looking for EPIC!

I'd NEVER – and I mean never – put on a large-scale event before, nor a small event for that matter. I had no idea how to go about it. So, like any practical woman (because we all have it in us) – I just started dreaming about what good could look like.

I looked around at the community of women I had at the time to see who I thought could provide amazing value and insights to an audience just like me. I reached out to different women, and one by one the momentum built. But there is one key person that I hadn't reached out to. I knew exactly who I wanted.

At the end of 2014, I started planning EPIC Summit, which was the first all-day business conference for women that The Connection Exchange, my new little business, was about to host. The Connection Exchange would be a space for smart, savvy, driven women to come together and where they would connect, exchange experiences, contacts, laughs, and support. I remember at the time thinking, *I have no idea how to put on an event, but how hard can it be?* Little did I know!

I had no experience and no idea what I needed. I had never dealt with a venue before, so I didn't know how to negotiate, get a better deal or collaborate. With an event on the other hand, I knew what I liked and what I didn't like, and so I asked myself what I would want. If I was going to pay $350 odd for an all-day summit, where would I want it to be? Circa sounded good, which is a stunning event venue overlooking the beach in St Kilda. What food would I want? A gorgeous feasting-menu-style spread, flowers on each table, goodie bags and cocktails post-event so I could spend more time getting to know the ladies I had spent the day with.

One thing I knew for sure was that if I ran a conference, there was one person I had to have as a speaker. That was Lisa Messenger, who was editor-in-chief of *Collective Hub* magazine, one of the fastest growing magazines for entrepreneurs in Australia and globally. I had no idea how to connect with her. So, like any normal person (so I thought) I googled her email address and sat down to write to my first speaker.

In my mind I thought, *If she says yes then the conference is on, if she says no then it was a good idea that would probably not go anywhere or something I could think about doing later.* When I emailed, I could have pretended to be cool, but I wasn't cool at all. I gushed, and I was so excited to be writing this email saying, "Lisa, I would love you to come and be the keynote speaker at EPIC Summit in Melbourne. This is my idea, and this is what I'm doing." And then outlined the who, what and where of the event. I was lucky enough that her marketing team connected, and it was a big yes! Obviously, a paid gig, but yes none the less, and I was off and running. From there, EPIC Summit was born.

With a wonderful team of two – Tahlia Meredith from The Melbourne Freelancer and Sarah Poppy from Sarah Poppy Design – I had put my dream event together.

Now I would love to tell you that everything ran smoothly, tickets sold like hot cakes and I made $50K, but that would be a lie. It was far from smooth sailing. There were tears – a lot of tears along the way – but I knew that I was on the right track. We had booked Circa in St Kilda, which is stunning. We had a great speaker line-up and I had a great team supporting me. The problem was – we weren't selling as many tickets as I needed to cover the forty-odd thousand dollar cost of the event. So, with nothing but determination to make this event a success – I hustled like I had never hustled before. I was getting ticket by ticket sold, speaking to people, connecting with other women in business communities, asking for what I needed. I had no brand in the market yet because we were just starting and I was in build phase, but there was no way I was about to lose this money, which was from our personal bank account. Not something I'm advocating you do, by the way.

This is where brand becomes your biggest asset. When you have a strong brand and relationships then it's easier to sell what you have because people come to you, follow you, buy what you have and want to support you. Whilst I had a small community and following, it wasn't enough to fill a conference room. I asked my speakers to promote, we were on The Collective website, we used Google AdWords, Facebook ads and more. No stone was left unturned and I was in too far to consider cancelling, and that was definitely not what I wanted to do.

It didn't occur to me that I was starting with no real brand reputation, but I thought I had the ace in my pocket with Lisa as our keynote and that everything would be fine. A lesson I learnt is that just because you love someone and you hold them on a pedestal doesn't mean that others know who they are or feel the same way. Whilst Lisa was definitely a drawcard, Collective was relatively new and didn't have the community or brand power it had later down the line. I definitely banked on that too much. I also assumed that everyone would see the ads or hear about the event, and even though we spent $2,000 on paid advertising channels, there were still people who were upset post the event that they didn't know about!

About halfway through promoting the event, I realised that we may not break-even, so I contacted Lisa's team and asked if we could have her for the evening as well. I was honest and told them that I wasn't going to break-even. I think sometimes we try and play it cool, and if we're honest, people understand and if they can help they will. We were flying her in and putting her up at the hotel at Circa, buying loads of her new books to sell at the event, and so they said yes and the second event on the same day was born.

If the day conference wasn't going to break-even then the evening event was another opportunity for people who couldn't make it for the day but wanted to come to "An Evening in Conversation with Lisa Messenger" later that night. That meant 125 tickets at $125 – and that was our saving grace! It was the one thing that meant we broke even on the night plus book sales from her two latest books that we bought wholesale and sold retail, which attendees could then get signed. Lisa was amazing and totally earned every cent that day if not more!

On Wednesday 4th March 2015, we held our first EPIC Business Summit with 88 women in the day and 125 in the evening. It was exhilarating, exhausting and expensive, but we broke even, had taken the business brand to a whole new level, and now had the reputation for beautiful events that were practical for women in business.

Like I said, this was the first event I had ever run, so the learning curve was so steep, and I could not believe what we had achieved. I was fortunate to have Jade McKenzie from the Event Head as my event coach, talking me off the ledge every time I thought, *What have I done? I can't believe how much money I've invested in this. I can't believe where we're at.* For some reason I thought it would be better to learn how to run the event myself rather than outsource the event management. When I look back, I wish I had outsourced, but then again, I learnt so much along the way – it was just a very painful way of learning!

EPIC Summit was the beginning of bigger things. Once I built the community, I could see that the women we were attracting were exactly who I wanted it to be, and I'm so lucky to still attract those women today into our online courses, community and events.

After EPIC, so many people asked me how I pulled it off – it was the focus and the realisation I was in it, boots and all, and I had to make it a success.

The more I do big things in my business, the more I've realised that I use a little formula I like to call D.R.E.A.M.

D is for dream. What do you want? How would it look if you had no limitations? What would it do for your business? How could you make it happen? This is just you having fun, going wild and seeing what comes out of it. That was where I started with the first EPIC Summit. I asked myself if I could have it anywhere – where would I have it. The answer at the time was Circa. If I could have anyone as my keynote, who would it be? The answer was Lisa. What food would we have, what goodie bags, what else… Have no limitations, just go with everything that comes to mind.

R is for research. Now I want to just point something out here. At this stage you haven't committed to anything, you're just seeing what it could look like. You're just playing with ideas. I called Circa and I asked for a price, I checked what else I would need on the day like AV, food, drinks, etc. I found out how much Lisa's fee would be to speak at the event plus other costs. I created a spreadsheet to look at total costs and how much tickets would need to be to cover costs. This is about working out the viability of what you want to do. What will it cost to create, how much do I want to make, how many people will we need and what must I do to get the ball rolling.

E is for explore. I called a few other venues, checked different suppliers to make sure that I was getting a good price, plus I was learning so much about how everything works. When you explore, you're also moving your mindset into – this is possible. It could happen, do you have the resources available to you if you move ahead? This quickly and with no commitment gives you an overview of what's possible.

A is for ask. I talked to potential speakers and I sent off the email to Lisa. Once again, at this stage I'm just asking a lot of questions. If I go ahead, great, if not, then that's okay too. Asking for what you want in life and business is a great skill to have or develop. My mum always used to say – if you don't ask you don't get, and that's never left me. When you ask questions, you can also see what else is possible. Is there the opportunity for collaboration? Can you get something free or with a discount? Lisa was promoting *Daring and Disruptive* and *Love and Life* at the time, so I was able to purchase books at wholesale and then sell them at the event and have her sign them, which meant additional revenue opportunities.

M is for make it happen. So, now you know what good looks like, you've researched what you need, you've explored different options, you've asked and it's time to decide if you're in or out. With everything you now know about making your dream a reality, what will you do? I find that if you've gotten to this stage then you're usually ready to jump in. Had you started researching and realised there was no way you could make it happen, you would have stopped well before now.

So often we start with ideas and then kill them before they've had a chance to breathe. Using the D.R.E.A.M. method allows you to explore ideas and validate them without financial commitment. It also helps you learn along the way. While researching EPIC Summit, I learnt so much more than I ever expected, which set me in great stead for when we ran EPIC Summit 2016 with Emma Isaacs as our keynote.

"TODAY
I WILL
CHOOSE TO
SHOW UP."

Chapter Seven

THE COURAGE TO PLAY BIG

100% believe that your success or failure depends on how focused, committed and strong your mindset is to achieve what you want to achieve. There may be people who believe something different, but when I listen to the hundreds of stories like JK Rowling, Gary Vee, Tony Robbins and Marie Forleo (just to name a few), they all started in very humble beginnings. Not middle class, university educated and cash-backed businesses – but grit, determination and hard work. So that's where we will start.

Mel Robbins said, "Confidence isn't the assurance of a successful outcome, it's the willingness to try."

So, how do you gain the courage to play big?

Before we start this journey together there are some key things I want to share with you.

When most of us start our businesses, we deal with thoughts that hold us back. In my 50 interviews, a word I kept hearing was 'safe'. What does safe ensure? It ensures we need not do more work, take the risk of finding out what others will say or think and it also means we don't have to own our ideas and our talents because by staying safe, we're not putting ourselves, our ideas, our products and services out there – so no one can criticise them.

Whether you're just starting or you've been in business for a while, there is ALWAYS a next level you can play at to take your business even further. So, whether you're earning $10k or a million dollars – either way, your mindset and clarity of where the next step is for you and your business is what we want to focus on.

What does playing big mean? No matter what it means for you – to me, playing big is the confidence and clarity to do the things you want to in your business. It's going for the big things you dream about and you want to achieve. Playing big looks different to different people, so you're here to run your own race; don't worry about anyone else – you just DO you!

One of the biggest tools to help you play bigger is clarity – clarity of vision, focus, offering and audience is where you can target what you're doing and how you're doing it. This isn't just about knowing who your ideal client is, it's about knowing yourself, what your strengths and weaknesses are and how you will operate and manage yourself during the time you work in your business. And, to be honest, the times you're not working in your business as well.

Once I knew exactly who my ideal client was, what I was here to do and nailed my service, offerings, packages, and pricing – it all came together. And that's what I want you to feel and walk away with.

So, how do you get that clarity? It's through knowing what you want and what lights you up. Where you serve people best and what they respond to the most when it comes to the things you do.

One of the exercises I do with my students in Brand Builder's Academy is a deep dive questionnaire. It helps you dig into what you're doing, what you're thinking, how you're feeling – so you can know when you're holding yourself back and what to do when that happens.

If you can recognise your resistance, understand why it's happening then work through a plan to move yourself through it, you'll be amazed with what you're capable of.

I'm so aware of my own mindset these days that I can catch myself in half a second when I'm resisting something. To give you an example, I wrote Brand Builder's Academy months before I launched the first time around. I wanted to give myself loads of time to create, prepare, market, etc. And then there came a point where I just wasn't doing the work I knew I was supposed to be doing. I would literally sit on the couch and my husband would ask, "How's it all going?"

I would say, "It's not going great because I'm in resistance." So, I allowed myself to be in that for a few days, then I kicked my own butt, booked out time in my diary and sat down and did what I knew I needed to do. It's only through being honest with yourself about what's going on that you'll be able to move through it.

Firstly, you have to look at your own responses when you're in resistance. Being honest and identifying your behaviours and beliefs and how you handle different situations, pressures and habits is one of the key skills you have to learn and use often. Before you can play a bigger game, you must know exactly what's going on inside, so it's a good place to start.

Some of the questions you can ask yourself are:

- Do you feel that you're playing a big game in your business at the moment?
- If you were playing a bigger game – what would you be doing?
- How would playing big make you feel?
- What are your drivers or motivation?
- When you're not doing the things you know will help you move forward – what are you doing instead?
- What are your pressure points?
- How do you work best?
- When are you at your most confident?

We dive deeper into all this in the course, but I think these are great questions to start with.

Now some of these questions may bring up different things for you, but for you to work through them yourself and write down the answers will be a powerful exercise for you to do – so don't resist it. The other tip I have is to ask yourself the question out loud. When we internalise things they can seem less powerful, but when we say things out aloud it can bring them to life.

Digging into whether there is an issue around confidence or self-esteem or worth is another one to sit on.

If it's a lack of confidence, one of my big activities I love doing at the beginning of every year is to look at where my skill gap is. So, for example, I've hired a coach who specialises in B2B corporate work – getting more corporate clients – because that's an area I need to focus on. So, if you have a skill you need to build, something you need to learn, then plan it out, put the money aside for it and do what you have to do to build that skill.

If it's a lack of self-esteem, then you'll need to dig a little deeper here. Why don't you think you deserve what you're going after? Is it because a parent, teacher or friend said you won't be able to do it? Is it because you've never felt deserving? Is it because something happened in the past that has made you afraid to go after what you want?

Whatever it is, spending time working on shifting these blocks is a game changer. If you have sabotaged yourself again and again and you can't work out why, then there may be something here. What I don't want to do is brush over this because feeling deserving will be a huge positive when you're wanting to play big – because you know that you deserve the success it can bring.

If you put offerings together and then don't put them out there – why? These are questions I would love you to answer. Once again, being honest with yourself is where you will acknowledge the problem and power the shift.

To grab the free downloadable for this section on how you can PLAY BIGGER, head to

www.playbigbrandbold.com/resources

Branding

BOLD

—

"PEOPLE WILL
LOVE YOU AND
PEOPLE WILL
HATE YOU AND
IT WILL HAVE
NOTHING TO DO
WITH YOU."

Chapter Eight

—

BRAND POWER BABY

The first time I experienced the power of brand was when I was about twelve years old and all I wanted was a Cabbage Patch doll. I remember my primary school friend Jade Foley had one and we were sitting in her room on the floor as she cradled her new doll and we were looking at the adoption certificate.

All my friends were buying them, but I didn't have one. I can't remember why, whether I didn't ask or I wasn't allowed, I have no idea. But as I sit here writing this, I can still remember the feeling. The face of the doll, the box it came in, the certificate, the fact that these dolls were everywhere. The thing is you couldn't just have another doll like it – it was this particular doll you had to have. This particular brand; it was like the Chanel of the kid's world at over $80 a pop, and it had status.

In 2004, whilst working for a big four consulting group in London, I worked with an external brand strategy team on a new recruitment campaign. The organisation already had a stellar reputation and formidable brand, but we were moving into a new era where we needed to attract a different type of person into the business, and so, with a very generous creative budget, we worked with the partners and some consultants to understand their differentiators. What made them stand out? What made their consultants different so we could share what they were about. In the end we landed on the strapline 'We work at the intersection of Think and Do'. Whilst that might sound simple, the team we were working with brought this to life in a very cool way using simple objects to power bigger ideas.

When we looked at their competitors in the market, McKenzie & Baine consulting used to provide strategic solution documents but wouldn't implement the project. Accenture, CapGemini and IBM would do a lot of the technical grunt work but not be as focused on high-level strategy; whereas the business I worked for would do the high-level strategy and then work with the client to implement the solution. They worked at the intersection of Think and Do – a key differentiator for them in their marketplace.

It was exciting to be part of creating their employer brand strategy and campaign and then executing it in a series of written copy, ads, creative, events and more. Their brand was already great, but we were building something different alongside it to strengthen what they already had, and the results were amazing. Whether they paid more or less than their competitors, people wanted to work for them because their brand position and unique differentiators were strong and spoke to the type of people they wanted in the business.

Whether you're seven, twenty-seven or forty-seven years old, we all have a pull towards certain things. The brands we use or engage with say something about us. They say something about who we want to be, where we see ourselves in the world and how we want to show up. Even being a 'non-brand' person says something about your personal brand. If you use natural deodorant you made yourself or you shop at places that only sell unpackaged, organic goods – that says something about you too. Brands have become part of our lives and, most of the time, part of our identity.

I've always known that I've liked nice things, and I learned in my 20s as my earning power grew which brands set me apart or made people look at me differently. My girlfriends and I used to go to the designer shoe warehouse sales in London when I lived there. There would be a queue up the block on New Bond Street. You'd rush in and run to the section with your size stuck on the wall, and then you'd trawl through the Stella McCartney, Jimmy Choo, Manolo Blahnik and all the rest. You'd buy things that weren't that comfortable, but it looked good and you had 'the brand' that you knew mattered! Sad but true – and when you're in your 20s you can be that frivolous.

I always say to my Brand Builder's Academy students and to my community – people buy what they want to BE, DO or HAVE.

Your brand will make someone feel a certain way and you need to know what that is. Many of the women I meet want to be bolder, want to do bigger things and they're on their way or journey to build the courage, and I'm part of that journey for them. They want to be more organised, strategic and focused on achieving what they want. They want to Play Bigger and they want to Brand Bolder (funny that!). They want to stand out from the crowd and be seen as different. They are passionate doers. They want to **BE** bold; they want to **DO** things that matter and will move them forward, and they want to **HAVE** a business that is sustainable and growing.

If you wrote down what your customers want to BE, DO and HAVE, what would that say or look like? Do you know?

I know where I need to position my brand and what my differentiators are. It's always worth the time and effort to know yours inside out too!

1. BRAND POSITIONING

I still find it amazing when I talk about brand so many people still think it's the logo and colours or the look of your business.

One thing I think a lot of small business or soloprenuers forget to think about is where they want to position their brand in the market. If you're not exactly sure what I mean – my question is, would you expect to pay $1000 for something at Target? Would you expect to pay $10 for something at Tiffany's? Each business has positioned themselves at a specific place in the market.

Target is affordable lifestyle, clothing and family goods that are stylish and accessible – but affordable is part of their positioning. People know who Target is for, what it delivers and you know the type of person that shops there. The same goes for Tiffany's or Chanel. You're not going to be heading in there for an afternoon shop with your loose change, and once again, we know what kind of people we think shop there too. There may be different segments they target, but there is a general sociographic profile.

So, if you're a business owner then you need to be asking yourself – where do I want to play in the market. Who do I want to be associated with or in line with, and I'm not talking about your competitors – remember to always look to other industries for fresh ideas. One of the best books you can read to get your mind thinking in a different way is *Blue Ocean Strategy* by W. Chan Kim and Renée Mauborgne. I remember going to a breakfast years ago, and the person was talking about the book and the concept of Blue Ocean Strategy. Basically, it's when you're not competing with your usual competitors, but you've carved a space out for yourself that is so different that you can charge a higher price because there is no one like you.

The example they use is Cirque du Soleil. Even though they were technically a circus, they had no animals, their venues were amazing, the experience was something completely different and they charged 10 times the price of a normal circus ticket and people would pay it. They were competing against a higher positioned product like the theatre rather than a common circus. If you think about how you can do things differently that means you're not in competition with like-for-like but you're taking your business and ideas to a whole new level. That's when you're swimming in a blue ocean. When you're competing on price and other low-level factors then that's a red ocean, because blood is in the water.

2. VISUAL BRANDING

So, this is the 'stuff' that everyone knows and what they think of the most when you say the word brand. It's the pretty things. The logo, colours, look and feel.

No matter the product or service, if I'm doing anything new in my business that is visual, Pinterest is usually the first place I head to. I have a secret or hidden pin board where I pin loads of things I love the look of. Different designs, fashion, inspiration – anything that appeals really. Then I share that with my graphic designer. The first time we were putting together the visual branding around one of my courses I basically said to Leanne, my designer – if Sunnylife and Gorman had a baby, that's what I want it to look like. I also shared my Pinterest inspiration board with her. The end results were what I wanted, and I loved it. It was bold and it stood out, which was perfect!

If you can draw on other brands as inspiration or provide a visual feast for your own designer to get creative with, that can also help you to get to an end point you love. The one thing I will say is that your visual brand, just like everything else in your business, will attract some and deter others and that's just the way it is. Knowing your audience and where you want to position your brand, as we've already discussed, is super important. We buy with our eyes most of the time and are attracted to things that appeal to us and who we see ourselves as.

3. BRAND PERSONALITY AND VOICE

Brand personality is basically how you want to show up in the world. Investopedia.com says, "Brand personality is a set of human characteristics that are attributed to a brand name. A brand personality is something to which the consumer can relate; an effective brand increases its brand equity by having a consistent set of traits that a specific consumer segment enjoys."

The end of that definition is important – it's a set of traits that a specific consumer segment enjoys. Your brand will attract or repel, depending on how you show up.

Whether you're a large organisation or a solopreneur, taking the time to define what your brand personality and voice will be is always important. You know when you read something a 'business' writes and it just speaks to you? You get their sense of humour, you understand their tone and you appreciate the way they communicate with you?

Well, that my dear, is tone of voice. It's how you speak to people through the written word, and it provides an insight into you, your business, how you want to be seen and how you like to connect and communicate with people.

Who would have thunk it? But yes, everything you write provides a feeling. Sometimes it's a good feeling and sometimes it's a not so good feeling.

Now not all businesses will have the same tone of voice (duh!) because obviously everyone is different and the way we communicate is different. So, working out not only what works for you, but what also works for your clients and how you want them to feel, respond and receive your messages and information is really where you need to start.

I always think it's good to review things and make sure you're 'on brand', which basically means you're not Jekyll and Hyde when it comes to the content you post – and voice is one of the most important things.

KNOW WHAT YOU'RE HERE TO SAY

If I asked you to describe how you communicate and how you want to connect with your audience, what are three words you would use? For me in The Connection Exchange, I want our brand voice to be:

1) *Fun and Real* – I love a laugh so it's super important that some of our posts have a sense of humour, share things I think are funny and just be me – which can be daggy at times, fun for our readers but also honest. Life isn't a highlight reel!

2) *Helpful and Supportive* – I'm a business coach and brand consultant so we need to provide helpful tips, respond and engage to and with our audience and support them to grow their business and brand too.

3) *A Story Seller* – When it happened, why it happened, what she said, what was great, who was there, how you can be part of it next time – yay!

So, write down three words you think describe what you want your brand voice to do/say.

If you're struggling with this, then think about how you would normally speak to people. What is your sense of humour, if you're planning on injecting some in? Do you have a certain way of expressing yourself that resonates with your audience?

I know you've heard it before, but people buy from people, and it's the people who I love online that I usually work with. It'll be something they talk about, how they say it and what they're about that draws me to them. It's their unique take on things.

Remember, your vibe attracts your tribe, so don't worry about trying to be for everyone. Create a brand you love, and the right people will find you! Be okay with being different – that's what you want in the end. If you sound like everyone else, then you'll just blend in.

Tips and Tricks – When I write my subscribers newsletter or my Instagram posts, I write it to someone. So, for example I'll write:

Hey (Sarah),

How's tricks? Are you ready for Christmas? I can't believe we've got a week to go. Have you done all your shopping, because I sure haven't?

Even though I may not be putting someone's name in there – as I'm writing my captions or newsletters, I'm writing it to one specific person.

LISTEN UP – YOUR BRAND VOICE HAS TO KNOW YOUR CLIENTS

I want you to picture yourself in a room full of your ideal clients. Got it? Think about how you're saying hello, how you're asking them questions or how you're sharing what's happening with you.

How do they want to be communicated with?

Now your brand voice obviously must be authentic to you and what you're all about – but if you want to work with a certain type of business or customer then having a brand voice that is jarring for them is seriously not going to be doing you any favours. You must be 100% true to yourself, and hopefully what is true to you will attract the clients you want to work with too, but this is where the difference may be.

If you're an agency-style business and you want a more serious tone of voice (for whatever reason) – maybe you're working with larger corporates and they respond better to a brand voice that is more formal, then that's a conscious decision you have to make.

Understand how they communicate. Which platforms are they on? For example, your LinkedIn tone of voice may be slightly different to your Instagram one if you are focusing on different audiences. What do they need from you? What are they saying and how are they saying it? This isn't about mimicking them, it's about talking TO them in a way they will respond to you.

CASE STUDIES AND EXAMPLES OF BRAND VOICES WE LURVE!

One thing I've learnt after going out on my own is to learn from some of the best in the biz. It's not about copying, it's about watching people who know their craft better than you do.

I've never been great with copy. I'm a typo queen (sad to say, really) and have always been a big picture girl rather than down into the detail. So, once I write something, it's like putting splinters under my nails for me to go back and proofread. I am learning to get better and I love reading and watching people who are awesome with copywriting – it is an important skill to have. So, if words are your thing then more power to you, I say!

SKIN CARE BRANDS NAILING THEIR BRAND VOICE

Frank Body and Go-To Skin Care are two of my favourite brands online. Why? Because their sense of humour nails it for me every time.

Go-To Skin Care by Zoë Foster Blake is funny, silly and tongue-in-cheek. Just reading their product names and about page, you'll quickly understand what I'm talking about.

Here is an excerpt from Go-To Skin Care website: *"It was founded by Australian beauty editor and the author of Amazing Face, Zoë Foster Blake, (there she is there on the right, clearly thrilled to get her mug on the site) who has been in the beauty industry for 213 years, and is the result of years spent reviewing and using every kind of skin care product available, from supermarket to spa brands, and receiving invaluable feedback from women on what they like, don't like, and find utterly baffling about the products they use on their skin."*

To me it says – this is for the woman who just wants simple, easy, not too fancy, fun and accessible skincare. I will not bamboozle you with all the fancy beauty terms – if you want to get the makeup off your face then use our 'Properly Clean' or 'Very Useful Face Cream' – love it! Simple and easy with a bit of fun thrown in for good measure.

Frank Body uses their #letsbefrank hashtag which clearly shows you that they don't beat around the bush. These ladies are amazing when it comes to wordsmithing clever, funny and sassy word styling. They are speaking to a certain type of girl who likes to (probably) play hard, look after herself but with not too much muss and fuss – "I make natural skincare for the days you don't want to touch your legs and have them feel rougher than your last hangover." – so good!

STILL STRUGGLING? PERSONA IT!

If your brand was a person who would it be? Now I know the obvious answer that most people would give is – YOU. But like I said, not every brand will be exactly the same as the business owner and that's okay. Because my brand voice is me, it's easy to describe what I'm like, how I talk, what I like to talk about, what's funny to me and what stories I think are important. My brand attracts my coaching clients and the women who are in our community and I love them – they are exactly the women who I want to be hanging out with when it comes to my business and what I do.

If you're a little shy and you need a persona to show up (seriously no judgement here – if Beyoncé can do it – so can you, girlfriend!) then you do what you need to do. Personas are not a new thing. For anyone who loves a bit of Beyoncé, there's the famous story that she's actually really shy and so when she gets on stage, her persona Sasha Fierce – how awesome is that – takes over. Sasha Fierce is what you see on stage. It's the attitude, the steely look, the booty grinding goddess. So, every time she gets on stage this persona is her performer to help her to deliver the best show she can. And it's the same for you. Your persona can help you show up in a different way.

Create your brand persona. Who is she? What is she like? What is she here to do, say, be and how can you invoke her when you're writing your copy and creating your online magic? If she was going out on a Saturday night or out with friends for Sunday bunch, where would she go, what would she wear, what kind of jokes or conversation would she share? Get into the nitty-gritty of your brand persona so that you can really bring it to life.

Personas are great if you have other people working on your copy and content. If you can describe who your brand person, tone and voice is, then it makes it a lot easier for them to replicate it in the right way.

The only word of warning I would say is that if your brand personality online is completely different to your in-person brand, that is, when people meet you, then it can feel a little disjointed.

I can't be big, bold and crazy online and then when people meet me, I'm so different that they think I'm an impostor. So, use personas wisely. Miss B can still carry it off when she's in person even though she is shy, but she picks and chooses when she brings out Sasha Fierce.

4. BRAND EXPERIENCE

This is one of my favourites! I still remember going to The House of Elemis in London when I was 27 – that's a long time ago by the way! I was with my bestie, Karen, and we were getting a treatment done and then heading out for dinner. Without going into every single detail, it's still an experience I talk about to this day. From the minute I walked in, the people, place, and experience blew me away, and I felt like a million bucks just being there – it was amazing to say the least. We had a Moroccan mud experience where we went into a private dome that looked like we had been transported to Morocco. There was a selection of muds we rubbed on ourselves, there was music, exotic scents and more. As we sat there in that dome on what was basically two thrones, the steam rose, and I could feel every pore on my body open and my muscles melted away. After sitting there for what felt like an hour in a state of pure bliss, the water fell like rain from the dome ceiling and washed the mud away. I kid you not – it was amazing.

Once clean, we were able to have a shower and use all their body oils, which were infused with scented oils that made me want to eat my own arm. Karen and I emerged from that place and had dinner at a gorgeous little restaurant across the lane way, and we just kind of sat there in a haze of bliss and amazement.

That, my dear, is Brand Experience.

Something I'm still talking about 15-odd years later! From the moment I walked through the door to the minute I left, every single moment, every single person I came into contact with enhanced my experience.

Whether you work with your customers online or in person – crafting your brand experience is something I bang on about all the time. Don't leave it to chance, don't think that it'll take care of itself – you want to make sure that you have thought about all the things.

So, look at your website experience, the buying experience your clients go through, your onboarding and off-boarding of clients, the feedback process. I was sitting with a client the other day talking to her about live events, and I talked about walking through every minute of the customer experience. From the sales page, to the ads, to the ticket purchase, to the days leading to the event and the event on the day. Think about where they will park their car or catch public transport from, in relation to the venue. Are they on their own – what can you do to make them feel more welcome? What is lunch and coffee going to be like. If you know anything about Melbourne, we're the coffee snobs of the world, so just know that if you serve instant coffee, your name is mud! I personally don't do sandwiches because I hate sandwiches at an event. But think about the price of the ticket, or service or product, and think about what your customer will expect when they work with you. Brand experience is what people talk about. Having an experience that people talk about, love and come back again and again for, is super important and can be a huge benefit to your business.

Now, obviously a rockstar experience can mean different things to different people and understanding your audience makes all the difference. What my audience may love may be different to what your audience wants from you!

Personally, a rockstar experience consists of a number of things.

- Connect before they work with you and create a sense of value and excitement – you can call it desire.
- Ease of access and use – Make it easy for customers and clients to find and engage you. I can't tell you how often I have gone to a website to find out more about working with someone, only to click away in frustration.
- Make them feel amazing when they work with you, which hopefully makes them want to come back again and again.
- Think about the relationships after you've worked together to ensure they are out there being your biggest brand ambassadors!

Working through how you can surprise and delight your customers, giving them a great experience above and beyond what you've promised, is always going to leave a great impression they will talk about long after you've finished working together!

5. BRAND LOYALTY – BUILDING CUSTOMER LOYALTY

There is a saying: it's easier to keep an existing customer than it is to get a new one. This is where customer loyalty comes in, and taking time to build customer loyalty will always be worth your time! Here are nine ways to build customer loyalty in your business.

1. REWARD LOYAL CUSTOMERS

A famous CEO once said, "If you have customers that have been with you for a very long period of time, they should be made to feel important or to have a greater status in your business as befitting their patronage."

- Invite these loyal customers to previews of upcoming services or sales
- Occasionally give them discounts
- Compile data on customer birthdays and send birthday cards

These are things that can easily be done and cost little but can make a huge difference, so think about how you can reward loyal customers.

When it comes to business success, customers are everything – without them you don't have a business and they hold the key to your business growth. So, don't treat your customers like a number – think about how you can continue to build the relationship for long-term customer satisfaction.

2. SURPRISE THEM OCCASIONALLY

Giving your customers occasional surprises goes a long way in ensuring that they remain loyal to you. You may decide to give them rewards occasionally or invest in other creative ideas and surprises.

For example, I send out thank you cards and chocolate bars or books depending on what my clients like and what is right for them. If they aren't expecting it, then obviously it's exciting and surprising and positions me as different and someone who is thinking about them.

3. GIVE WITHOUT EXPECTATION

Giving without expectation can be hard. We're here to build and run a business, not a charity, but the more you give and help people, the more it comes back to you. As I've said before, you must be smart about what you're doing but don't underestimate your breadcrumbs. If you lay out the breadcrumbs, you'll eventually get to the gingerbread house where all the good stuff is!

4. FAMILIARITY

If you want a customer to be loyal to your brand, you must establish a sense of familiarity. First, make your brand approachable, like a friend, and that means personalising your brand. Your brand should have a welcoming character that's strongly presented across multiple channels, and its character should be consistent.

Any deviation in your brand voice could be jarring and create distrust, so don't neglect the consistency factor.

5. GRATITUDE

Customer-brand relationships are founded on a principle of logical exchange. Customers continue paying you money because they expect an equal value in return, whether that value comes in a product or service or an experience.

When you give your customers more than they're expecting or something that outweighs their perception of an "equal" value exchange, they'll feel gratitude toward you. And the more gratitude they feel, the more they'll want to stick with you. Find little ways to spark these feelings of gratitude.

6. BELONGING

One of the best ways to ensure customer loyalty is to make your customers feel that they're truly a part of something when they engage with your brand. Statistics show that brands who allow their customers to engage with them and others in their community experience 30% more brand loyalty. It also creates stickiness.

The key to making customers feel that they belong to your brand is create a sense they are part of something bigger than them. Think about how you can spark conversation, get opinions out there and see how the conversation can evolve and connect people in your community.

7. ESTABLISH A PERSONAL RELATIONSHIP
WITH EACH INDIVIDUAL CUSTOMER

A big part of customer loyalty comes down to your likability. People will almost always remain committed to a brand if they believe they've developed a genuine and mutually beneficial relationship. Take advantage of any opportunity to get to know a client on a personal level. I know the women in my community. I know about their families, holidays, what's going on with their lives – but not in a weird way, in a way that is connected. It's what being part of community is about.

8. LISTEN MORE THAN YOU TALK

If you've followed me for a while, you'll know that I always say listen more than you talk! Listening to your clients and customers is where you can evolve your business in a way that can almost guarantee customers. As they say, don't create products and then look for customers, build products that your customers are asking for. I had a number of clients ask if there was any other way to coach with me as they couldn't afford the one-on-one coaching – so I created courses. Many workshops I've run have been through request.

Creating customer loyalty through listening is a great way to continue to include your clients in the growth and development of your business.

When you find clients that love what you do then they love being part of that process.

9. RECOGNITION

Who doesn't love to be recognised? Talking about your customers to other customers, referring them and singling them out when you can are also great ways to make them feel special and valued. As customers and clients, we want to matter, feel valued and want people to appreciate that we're here and we're engaging and being part of what they are creating. It matters to us and it's easy for businesses to do this whether they are big or small. Remember, it's when we focus on the things that matter that we can make special things happen.

How can you recognise your clients more? Putting these things in place earlier rather than later is also a great thing to do.

For creating a rockstar experience – connection is everything – people want to be seen and they want to feel that you care.

Working through a customer experience roadmap from go to woe is always useful and something I do at least once a year to make sure that from the minute someone finds me through Google or my socials, it's a good and easy experience.

Make your customers feel something unique and special and they will always remember you!

"YOUR
STORIES
MATTER."

Chapter Nine

———

STORYTELLING AND STORYSELLING

" I t is a human need to be told stories. The more we're governed by idiots and have no control over our destinies, the more we need to tell stories to each other about who we are, why we are, where we come from, and what might be possible". The amazing Alan Rickman (Snape in Harry Potter for those who don't know the name) once said this and I couldn't agree more.

I'm sure that as a child some of your oldest memories are of being told stories of your family, classic books by Roald Dahl or Dr Seuss – we read these to our kids even now. I remember my dad making up stories at bedtime or telling me about his childhood where there were 10 children. A tyre inner tube was their toy or a spinning top they had whittled out of wood. I'm still laughing a little because I'm sure you have those stories that your parents used to tell you too about walking to school in snow 'this high' (motioning their hand up to their knees) with no shoes... ah the good old days!

If the truth be told, *Play Big, Brand Bold* at its heart, is about storytelling. Well, storytelling and doing big things that may make you feel slightly nauseous! The joy of business hey? It's a mindset of building your business with a sense of adventure, fun and a little bit – or sometimes a lot

– of courage! It's about not taking yourself too seriously, understanding that you'll probably fail a lot before you're successful and being okay with that. When you're building a brand it's like being in a lab, which is why my podcast is called *Brand Builder's Lab* – I thought it was the perfect name! You test and try things out and see what works, what explodes, what fizzles out, but you figure out what's right for you. No one built a great business or an epic brand without making mistakes along the way. Just remember Coca-Cola only sold 25 bottles in its first year! But as we go through this journey it's the stories that make it come to life. It's the stories that help us share our message and lessons along the way. It's the stories that your followers and audience want to connect with.

I feel like the art of storytelling has had a renaissance in a big way and is changing lives everywhere with the likes of TED talks, YouTube and podcasts. Over the last couple of years I've been fairly addicted to Audible – you know the audiobook app, and as it stands I probably have over 50 plus books in my library. Along with podcasts, it's the one thing I listen to almost on a daily basis as I walk my dog Beau, and I get lost in the words someone narrates to me through the two little black wireless earbuds cemented in each ear.

It might be inspirational, educational or could just be insightful and entertaining. I don't know about you, but as a business owner I am guilty of mainly listening to and consuming business content. So whilst some people may ask – "Do you ever really switch off, Suz?" I have to be honest and say that I don't want to. I love learning and growing and being connected to others who think differently and have something unique and special to share with me.

When it comes to great stories, think about books you've loved or speakers that you've been drawn to and why. Usually, it's because they've shared something with us – a funny story or an example of an experience. Stories are the things that we still remember years after it was first shared with us.

So back to Audible. There are three people who I could listen to all day long. Number one is Brené Brown – if you don't know her, then Google her, she's everywhere. I love Brené Brown. Like totally love her. I will consume everything and anything she puts out anywhere, any day, any time!

I think she is one of, if not the best speaker I've ever seen and listened to. I remember a number of years ago sitting on a bucket in front of my house painting our picket fence and listening for about six hours to her seminar on *The Gifts of Imperfect Parenting* and it's changed the way I parent. As she shared her knowledge and experience, it created a connection. She has no idea who I am but I feel connected to her, which also means that every time a new book comes out, I'm there buying and downloading it. She's not sharing the how-to, she's telling me powerful and life changing stories. She's challenging my thinking and she does it all through sharing amazing stories with humility, honesty and humor.

The second person is someone I've already introduced you to – Elizabeth Gilbert of *Eat, Pray, Love* fame and whose book *Big Magic,* as you know, was the inspiration for me to finish this book and now start penning my second and third books. Oh hello there Suz – the non-writer writer.

And the third is Shonda Rhimes who is the writer for hit shows like *How to Get Away with Murder, Greys Anatomy* and *Scandal.* She is also the author of one of my favourite books, *Year of Yes – How to Dance It Out, Stand In the Sun and Be Your Own Person.*

I get so immersed in what they are sharing, their stories and experiences that the lessons are so much easier to take in and sometimes I don't even realise that I'm learning as I'm listening. I recently had the pleasure of meeting Elizabeth Gilbert at an event in Melbourne. It was emotional for me to say the least. As she stood on that stage for an hour and a half and shared her stories, thoughts and experiences I just looked at her thinking – I just want to be around you more. I believe what you believe. It makes me feel more creative, like I can do so much more, like I have more to give.

Now confession time; because of all of those thoughts and feelings – yes the brand consultant in me did also think – if she was selling something today, I'm pretty sure I would be buying it. She wasn't selling anything but what I was really clear on, is that the power of storytelling can lead to very powerful storyselling. Remember that brand is the pull and marketing is the push. By sharing their stories they are building connection. And what is brand? It's the invitation to an emotional connection. It can be building trust, love, respect. It's your reputation and becoming known for something specific.

Whether you know it or not, your stories could be one of the most powerful brand strategies you implement. So the questions is, when it comes to building your business and your brand – what stories are you sharing? What are you giving your audience that allows them access to your world, your experiences, your past, your insights and the lessons they can learn from your journey?

How can you tell your story, or a story of your client, in a way that showcases what you do and how you helped? Humans are built to connect and be drawn to stories. It's how we pass on information and how we tell others where we've come from.

I want to share three different ways you could start to implement storytelling and storyselling in your business right now.

1) Your Brand Story
2) Micro moment story telling
3) Brand experience story selling

YOUR BRAND STORY:

Your brand story shares where you've come from, how you got here, why you do what you do and how I can now become part of that story. It doesn't need to be *War and Peace* but you want to convey what's important about what you're here to do and the person behind the brand.

So, I want you to think about how you share your story. This was something that took me a little while to get the hang of which is ironic because I do it for other businesses all the time. But when you do it for yourself, it's a different thing, so if you need to get help then get help developing this.

What do people want to know? It's sharing the story of why you're here, what inspired you, who you want to serve and what you want to leave as your legacy. Whether you sell widgets or dreams, your contribution, ideas, thoughts, struggles, successes and stories matter. As you read that sentence some of you may be thinking – *Why, why does my story matter? As if I can impact someone or something, as if I could create something big or small that matters.* But you know something – why not?

Imagine if the great leaders, influencers, activists and heroines of the world decided not to tell their stories. Imagine if they thought – *Why me? What's the point? There are so many other people out there.* Imagine if those with ideas that may have seemed just a little bit crazy thought – *It probably won't work.* The world is made up of people who do big things every day – and you, my bold action taker, can be one of them if you so choose!

If you can help, shape, encourage and lift even one person up and help them to follow their own path, then that is always worthwhile. So start to craft your story. Think about the moments that brought you to this place. Think about the lessons you've learnt and how you can use those in your content, videos, podcast, books, speaking – wherever you hang out.

Whenever I'm working with a speaker, coaching or personal brand strategy client, stories are one of the first things we work on. Anyone can teach content, but it's the stories we share with content sandwiched in-between that make our presentation unforgettable or memorable. So spend some time writing down all the stories that are relevant to your journey, what you talk about, share and teach.

MICRO MOMENTS STORY TELLING

As the second edition of this book has been published in 2020, right now Instagram stories has a huge amount of attention and traction and is the perfect platform for micro moment story telling. When it comes to building a brand, you have to become a storyteller. People aren't interested in the fake gloss anymore, they want the real and raw, the honest journey. We want to see the behind-the-scenes, what you're up to, who you're working with and what makes you tick.

Mid 2018 and at the beginning of 2019 I started to track my income specifically from Instagram stories. I was using stories regularly and enjoyed connecting with people so much more in the micro moments of our day rather than the Instagram feed. I'd get questions and I'd send back an audio direct message or video answer. Every time someone joined Brand Builder's Academy or bought a ticket to an event I'd send them a direct message in stories and connect with them personally.

By the end of the first quarter of 2019 I had attributed around $25,000 in sales to Instagram stories. People were either finding my podcast or seeing me speak at an event and then following me on stories to keep in contact. What I found is that once they found me on stories they were then taking action and booking in to work with me. A corporate client booked me for a presentation skills workshop with their team because their learning and development coordinator was one of my followers and saw me talking about the workshop one day.

I religiously ask clients not only where they heard about a product, service or event but I ask them – where did our relationship start? Was it the *Brand Builder's Lab* podcast? What it Instagram stories? Was it seeing me speak at an event? Knowing where people first found me and then where they got to know me has been super important to thinking about how I go about my brand and content strategy. I honestly feel that when you nail your brand and content strategy you don't have to spend as much time on the marketing.

The rule of thumb is that it takes around 18 touch points for someone to buy from you. But with platforms like Instagram stories someone can have 18 touch points with you over two to three days. I love it when someone says – *"Well someone isn't just going to meet you and then buy from you straight away"*. I actually have stories and case studies of that happening. When you create an ecosystem of content and real touch points, your ability to build trust through the micro content moments and storytelling is one of the most powerful things you can do, and if you're not doing it, then why not?

BRAND EXPERIENCE STORY SELLING

I'm so nosey. Let's be honest – given half the chance most of us are. When it comes to people we like and follow or events we have total FOMO (fear of missing out) over, then we want to see what's happening, who was there and what it was like. One of the best examples of brand experience story selling, could be either an event experience that you want to share and showcase or it could be experiences that people get when they work with you or are part of your community. We buy things that visually appeal to us. Remember, we don't just buy a product, we buy into a community and an identity. We want to go to the event and be part of that tribe. We want to experience what those people who attended experienced and we'll pay for the opportunity to physically be there and now we'll also pay for the opportunity to virtually be there too.

When people ask me – "What do I post? I have no idea what to say. How can I 'create' content for stories?" My answer is always the same. I don't really 'create' content for stories – I just take you on the journey with me. I let you know what I'm doing, where I am, what I'm thinking, how I'm navigating interesting, insightful, challenging or fun things. I'm giving you insight into my life and business. You'll see the highs and the lows. You'll see me when I have incredible moments but I'll also share with you when I feel broken and I'm struggling. **It's the micro moments that build trust.** It's those micro moments that build connection. You are my community and I've chosen to make you part of my journey and take you with me on this ride. You can choose to hang out or you can choose to unfollow – the choice is yours.

What you may not realise, is that when you share the journey, people want to be part of what you do, what you offer, what you sell, where you're going to be speaking and basically whatever you're going to be a part of. I just really want to make sure that you walk away from this chapter understanding the incredible opportunity you have. This is the time to get real, raw, and honest, to connect and start sharing the brand experience that is you – it's your personal brand. What you stand for. What you're about. Why you do what you do. It has power. Don't forget it.

GREAT STORIES STAY WITH US.

Just in case you missed it the first time I said it – your story matters. Just know that you can create something from nothing and then give it meaning that people can connect with – the right people. The people who want what you have and connect with your story, the journey that you're on and where you're going. When I think of anyone and everyone that I admire, there is always a story I connect with behind the business and even though often we don't like to think about it as 'the brand', their success is because of the stories and impact they have made and shared. It's the experience they share that builds their brand and the connection people have with it. It's either their opinion, unique take or the way they look at or see the world. Don't you love meeting interesting people with different points of view? You have a viewpoint whether you realise it or not. It's okay for you to share it.

I was recently listening to an interview with Adam Braun, the founder of Pencils of Promise, a global 'for purpose' organisation that builds schools and educates children all over the world, which he started with just $25. He called the business Pencils of Promise because when he was travelling, he came across a young boy and asked him, "If you could have anything in the world, what would it be?" The little boy said, "A pencil". He didn't want toys or food or anything else – just a pencil. To that child it meant possibilities. He could draw anything he wanted and it made him happy. Those are the stories we remember.

Coco Chanel is famous for shaping the fashion industry but started with humble beginnings. She took something simple like clothing and created an iconic feeling of luxury, style, and confidence around the Chanel brand. Her quotes are in this book and all over the interwebs. Give people a feeling when they connect with your brand and they'll never forget you.

Michael Jordan gave Nike a story that young kids and old men could relate to. He lost as many times as he won but he never gave up. A brand is a feeling above all else. It's a connection we have personally with something or someone. It reflects something in us. As one person I may not be able to educate thousands of children around the world, but if I donate or support a 'for purpose' group like Pencils of Promise or a similar organisation and become part of that vision and the work they do, then I can make a difference and I get to be part of their story.

Within The Connection Exchange we support One Girl which is a charity that educates young girls in Africa and teaches them to run businesses so they don't have to get married at 13, and they can finish their education and stand on their own two feet – a life I could never imagine. But the point is with just $35 a month we as a business are doing something that matters. If your mission is to empower and support women for example, then ask yourself how far that mission can reach. Sure, The Connection Exchange is here to support women to build their businesses and we do that through the podcast, Brand Builder's Academy and events, but how is that mission going further, doing more, reaching others who can't afford or don't have the life opportunities we have? That's why One Girl was the perfect fit for our mission and also gives our business a wider and deeper purpose.

So I want you to start to think about the stories that you could be sharing, both in a bigger and a smaller way. Think of your brand story and the brand experience story selling you could be doing more of, as well as the micro moments of storyselling, to attract, engage and spark interest for your audience. Great stories stay with us, so start telling yours.

SIMPLE

MESSAGES

SELL

Chapter Ten

THE MAGIC IS
IN THE MESSAGE

After working with hundreds of business owners through coaching, events and courses, one thing always remains true in my experience. When a business owner is unclear of their message, what follows is usually a lack of direction, conviction, and confidence. It might sound simple, but I believe that the magic is in the message.

Whenever I think of anyone who I follow, respect, or have purchased from, I've known exactly what the outcome of working with them, listening to their podcast, following them on social, whatever they do, will be. I know what they are here to do, and I'm clear on what that means for me.

The key there is – what that means for me. I may be clear on what you're about, but if I have no idea what that means for me personally and what problem you're solving (once again) for me, then I'm not buying.

When you're clear on your message and brand, then the right people will find you. And not just find you but literally be jumping in the air saying:

"Thank goodness I found you."

"I've been looking for you."

"You're the one for me. Hallelujah!"

A few years ago, I went looking for a copywriter. Now I know a lot of copywriters that I've used for many personal and corporate jobs in the past but with me and my brand, I was looking for someone special. I wanted someone who made me laugh when I read their work; they were smart, funny and passionate. I was lucky enough to find said copywriter through a Facebook group I was in.

Her blog posts were shared, and I had a little read. As soon as I read her work, I knew I had found my woman and I said:

"Thank goodness I found you."

"I've been looking for you."

"You're the one for me. Hallelujah!"

When we find our people, we just know it, and if they stand out because their brand personality, voice, and positioning are right for me, plus they have the magic in their messaging, then I'm there with bells.

If I'm honest it's a relief – like pure relief that I've found the solution to my problem.

However, as with everything in life, your business, personality and the way you work will resonate with some people and won't resonate with others – and that's okay. That's one thing that Playing Big and Branding Bold is all about – being 100% fine with being you, standing out, and saying I'm okay with not being for everyone.

It's not up to you to be everything to everyone. Own your space, and your zone of genius. Be yourself and be authentic. Now I will not use the word authentic like everyone else – I will tell you what I mean by that. Authentic is "be yourself and not who others want you to be or who you think you ought to be".

Now, the majority of books, courses, etc., will tell you to know who your ideal client is, but I will break that down a little and take it a step further.

Obviously, if you know who your ideal client is then you'll know who they are, and hopefully you have at least five or so people who are real clients you can bring this to life around.

My ideal clients are Sam, Louise, Lisa, Katherine, and Leah. There are more of them I could name, but there is something specific about these women in my community that I base a lot of my business decisions on.

They are highly driven, intelligent, and creative women. They have all the smarts they need to do what they do amazingly well in their business, but there are elements of business which may be technical, content specific, pricing or other factors I can support them to do better. So, when someone says "who is your ideal client?", they are the women I think of immediately. They are also funny, great company, diverse in their thinking and caring. That's a bit of a bonus really!

If you already have or know this information, then you're in a powerful position to connect, influence and attract the clients you'd love to have.

The next step is thinking about who my dream clients are and then my cream clients. Now I can't take credit for this – I have no idea who coined this first, but I love it. Your ideal, dream and cream clients.

So, my ideal clients are the women I currently work with.

My dream clients are the ones that not only show up and are fully connected to me and my business and how we can work together, but they are also out there doing the work, shouting about what I do and what we do together and bringing others into the business. I must say that some of my ideal clients already fall into my dream client category.

Then there are the CREAM clients. These are the ones I have to pinch myself about. This could be a corporate training gig that's worth $50k or $100k where I'm working with them over a longer period of time supporting the people in the organisation to get confident, value their worth and build epic personal brands. They may be longer-term relationships or maybe it's someone who pays me $50k to speak at an amazing event and flies me business or first class wherever I'm going – a girl can dream you know! And maybe if I put it on my vision board then one day it won't just be a dream. I kinda get chills as I write that, if I'm honest, because why not? Why not me?

Why couldn't that be me on that stage? What's stopping me?

Name it, Claim it, and Frame it, I say!

So, with your magic message, what's at the core?

Well, developing your core message. Having a core message that is what you're known for. If you position what you're known for in the right way then your ideal, dream and cream clients know that you're for them!

It's what you stand for, it's what you want to share, it's that one big thing that when someone says, "I'm looking for an awesome PR person who can help me stand out" – they think of you and they recommend you because that's what you always talk about. It's your core message.

Whether you want to be a thought leader or not, if you want to passionately talk about what you do and what you believe in, then you need to know what that is.

People are drawn to and work with people who resonate with them; they love what you talk about, what you do and how you do it and they feel you can help them.

For me, it's about building 'Confidently Bold Brands' which is where *Play Big, Brand Bold* came from. It encompasses everything that I believe you need in businesses. Play big means – put your message out there confidently, connecting with people and showing up every day because that's what it takes. Brand bold means – be unique, have something you're seriously proud of and share it shamelessly.

So, what is that message for you? Or what, as I like to call it, is your 'neon sign'? What would you want flashing above your head when it comes to who you are and what you do?

A way you can work out your neon sign is to workshop ideas and words.

I usually mark out three columns on a whiteboard or page.

Column 1 – How do you want your clients to feel?

Column 2 – What are descriptive words you could use around what you do?

Column 3 – What do your clients say about you or how do they describe you? Why did they pick you is another good question to ask.

When you start to put all this down on paper, you'll start to see a theme or feeling.

For me the word that people kept using was they wanted to be more confident in how they were putting themselves out there. I personally believe that the way to do this, and my big desire for my clients to do, is to embrace 'bold'. Plus, that's how people described me when I asked them. 'You're so bold and confident and that's what I want to be'.

And Branding is what I do. That's where my neon sign – Confidently Bold Branding came from.

A little note on this is that it can take time. It might need to percolate, and you may have different iterations. You may create one and test it out, and it may work or it may not work. I had a client that created her neon sign that was super clear and powerful, and she actually attracted the exact client that the neon sign targeted – but she soon realised that wasn't actually the client she wanted. The good news – her neon signed worked. The bad news, it wasn't who she wanted to work with, so back to drawing board.

I get both big and small businesses that call me all the time saying "we want to be bold and we don't know how to be". So, the language you use is really important because it will connect and speak to people who really want that feeling, emotion, outcome.

I attended an event a while ago, and the speaker said your message can't be honed until it's witnessed. What that means is that every time you tell your story or talk about what you do – it gets more powerful. It doesn't work when it's just you saying it in your head. It actually takes you sharing it with others so you can see what they respond to and how they react, what they say, think and engage in. You can't do that by yourself.

Some people struggle to articulate what that is for them, but I honestly think it's just because they may not have spent time on it. You may know generally what you're about – what you want to do, how you want to help people, but to play a bigger game you must take a stand on something. Anything. Whatever is important for you. Becoming a thought leader or having an opinion on how things can be done is what attracts others.

Think about the people you follow and admire. What is it about them that makes you follow them or want to work with them? It's because they believe in something. They share that message freely and passionately and they invite you to buy and be part of what they are doing and offering.

That is the power of a clear and passionate core message, never to be underestimated.

Now if you have a core message and you're killing it in your business, but you want to play bigger, then my question is how can you amplify that to a wider market? Can you broaden your reach through targeted marketing, can you build strategic alliances or partnerships with other big players in the market? I see loads of big business cross-selling all the time with people whose brands align with theirs or who are offering work for similar audiences.

So, how can I develop my core message, I hear you ask?

Well, some questions I would work on are:

1. WHAT ARE YOU HERE TO DO?

Don't just think of the functional thing you do. You might say I'm here to make cookies and cakes – but what you're actually here to do is create magical experiences and beautiful and delicious things that are usually part of a celebration.

2. WHAT DO YOU BELIEVE?

What is your opinion on what people must do to succeed or achieve what you're talking about?

Take a stand – write down everything that you believe and why you believe it. Once again, we're doing conscious work. Not just throwing things out there but really thinking about why we believe what we believe and why it should matter to other people, because this is the magnet that will attract your tribe and ideal client.

3. WHAT ELSE MATTERS WHEN IT COMES TO THIS TOPIC?

So, these are your content pillars. I talk about getting your head in the game to play big, but lots of other things are important as well like core message, building community, developing partnerships, etc. Your core message is the overarching umbrella that everything else sits under.

It doesn't need to be complicated; we want to keep it simple. If you can focus on these three questions, you'll be able to narrow down that one core message you believe in.

Once you find that message – you'll never run out of things to talk about, because there are so many angles you can cover. Look at your offshoot topics, break them down even more and never assume that everyone knows what you know, because they don't.

One of the biggest barriers to your marketing or sharing what you know is that you assume that people know what you know. Hello, curse of knowledge, which is where we assume everyone knows what we know – because of course, they have been doing exactly what we've been doing for the last 10–20 years right?

The other thing that stops you from sharing your message may be that you think you've said it before, or someone has said it before. Do you think that everyone who has ever followed you or will follow you heard you talk about that one topic – that one time at 2pm on a Tuesday back in March? I'm guessing not.

Also remember that it takes you saying something several times, in several ways, before someone really hears it. Several years ago, I had one of my fabulous community tell me after two years she didn't realise I did pricing and packaging and brand positioning – which is key to what I do with most of my clients. I think I talk about it all the time, but a lot of people didn't know that – so I need to talk about it more and so do you.

Don't assume people know or are listening all the time. It's your job to reiterate it again and again and it's fine if they hear it 100 times as long as you're adding value along the way. Remember you want to become KNOWN for what you do, how you help people and what you believe.

By having a core message, plus all the other topics that surround that core message, you're reinforcing what you do again and again. If you're wondering where your clients will come from, I want you to understand that the more you share what you do and how you do it, the more people will associate or think of you first when that problem arises for them. You're the person they will think of when someone else asks who they know that does X.

Your core message also needs to align with your vision, mission and values. Any unique statements or content you can use or share with your audience. If you're able to work out a neon sign that explains in a sentence what you're here to do and who you're here to serve, then that consistency and clarity of message is what will stick with people. By saying this consistently and everywhere that we communicate, it means that people know exactly what we're about. There is no ambiguity on what I'm here to do, what I provide and what you'll get if you connect with me. Keep it simple and on point and you can't go wrong. Articulate your message as best you can. Sit down and work through it because repetition is the key to cutting through the noise and building your brand.

Just remember that it may take a while to come, but the words will eventually find you and stamp themselves on your business and brand and it'll just feel right.

SHARE

YOUR

GOODIES

Chapter Eleven

MARKET LIKE
YOU MEAN IT

One of the biggest barriers I've found for many women I've spoken to for Playing Big and Branding Bold is that they're self-conscious about what people will say if they put themselves out there, to the point where it stops them in their tracks. So, let's look at the mindsets that hold you back and let's take the ick out of marketing.

Often you may be worried about what people will say, that they won't be nice, you're worried you have nothing of value to say or that you'll stuff up in some way.

Some women I spoke to said things like:

"Because I've tried a few different things, I think people won't take me seriously."

"Maybe no one will be bothered to read what I write."

"What if I make no money?"

"People will think I look/talk/sound funny."

We have all these stories going on in our heads and it paralyses us into inaction.

There are a few different layers to break through in this section, so we will get to work.

A lot of times we feel embarrassed when marketing because we're worried that people say or think we're being salesy and pushy. I remember one occasion where I was teaching at a workshop the importance of using your images across your social channels and generally in your marketing. Someone said that she always thought people would look at her if she did and think she was being self-centred or 'look at me, look at me'. When I asked her if she thought that of me when I used my photos for marketing. She said no, she loved it!

So, the first thing is acknowledging the thoughts we have and realising that most of the time they aren't true. When I asked the women I interviewed what they thought people would say, and then asked if anyone had actually ever said that – the answer was no.

So, stuff comes up from our childhood. If our parents said things to us or teachers or mean girls or sisters or ex-work-colleagues – whoever – just know that a lot of these thoughts come from our past or from stuff we make up in our own heads, how we read situations and people and how we interpret what's going on.

Experiences and thoughts can come up from ages ago that you may not even realise are still there. When asking someone if confidence or self-worth was holding her back, it brought up a story of something that had happened 10 years ago, and she said she didn't realise that it was still a thing for her. These experiences might be from people either not in our circle anymore or they aren't our target audience.

Now if you have family or friends who don't support you in your business there are a few things you can do.

Firstly, you can either remove them from your headspace (which I know isn't easy), and what I mean by that is that you just don't talk to them about what you're doing – you protect your space.

Or as I've advised many women before – you may need to get brave and have the conversation that you would appreciate their support. Now sometimes partners can be our hardest gig. They see your business as a hobby, as something just occupying your time, but it hurts your feelings and discourages you if they aren't taking you seriously and supporting you.

I remember having this conversation with my hubby and made it very clear that my business was important to me and my goal was to do big things with it. Actually telling him my intention meant that he knew how serious I was and that it wasn't okay to comment about my business. Saying that, he's always been supportive and great. Often, they don't mean it to be nasty; sometimes they just see a job that isn't with a big company as not being serious.

When it comes to worrying about what people will say – it's up to you to set them straight.

Unfortunately, there will be those who hold you back because of their own insecurities and their lack of willingness to step out and do something that is risky or they see as scary. You're doing something that many people would not be willing to do. And I want you to acknowledge that. It's big – you are already doing big things – things that others aren't willing to do. So, give yourself a pat on the back for being brave!

Once again, we're being conscious – so spend some time writing down what you think people will say.

Then ask yourself if anyone has ever said that, and if it matters. There are a handful of people whose opinion matters – so don't let people who do not affect your life influence what you do. If you haven't watched Brené Brown's Man in the Arena talk on *99U* on YouTube, then do. She talks about how people in the cheap seats are the ones who always have a go – but they aren't in the arena with us doing the hard work, so they don't get to have a say. It's brilliant and one of my favourite talks of hers.

Secondly, once you acknowledge what you think will happen, I now want you to think about what you really want for your customers and community. What do you want to share with them?

What are their needs and how can you help them?

The reason we don't market ourselves confidently is because we're focusing on ourselves. Worried about how we look, how we sound, what people will think about us... and we're not actually focusing on our audience and customers.

When you focus on them and what you can share with them and help them with, the focus isn't on you anymore. By shifting your focus off you, it means you can respond to what they need.

One of the great side effects of getting over yourself is that it allows you to connect with people. They see what you're about. They hear your core message. They understand why you're different and you attract the right people.

If you're worried about how to get clients – this is how. This is how you put yourself out there and support people to do the things that you're great at. So, think about two or three key things clients ask you all the time and then let's work together to help you get that message out there.

Let's talk about my secret mindset when it comes to marketing! Are you ready for it?

I call it sharing. Now don't laugh, I know it's simple but it's always the simple things that work. I rarely think about marketing. I actually changed my mindset around what I do in my business by thinking about how I can share what I have. See – simple but effective if you're worried about being salesy.

Every time I have an event or I have an offer – I think, if I can help someone to play bigger, have a better brand, to get their pricing and packaging sorted so it makes it easy for people to work with them, then I know I've done a good job that day and I haven't 'marketed' AT them, I've shared what I believe WITH them.

I would encourage you to think about and focus on your client. It makes connecting with potential clients so much easier.

Another reason many of the clients I connect with don't like marketing themselves is because they don't love what they're putting out there visually. If you have a visual brand you love then it makes it even easier because you love putting your branding, images, photos, etc., out there.

I believe it's important to have good images of yourself, because you are your brand and people connect with you when they see you. They feel like they get to know you. I always say to clients they need to use their image in their subscriber newsletter headers so when you write and people are reading your updates, they're picturing you. It also builds a sense of familiarity, and the more familiar I feel with someone, the more likely I am to build trust quickly and then buy from them. So, there is method in my madness.

Now if you're not emailing your subscribers then you're missing a big opportunity to build a relationship with them, offer value and get more clients. I always ask where people hear about me for events, coaching, anything and often it comes from my newsletter as well as social and word-of-mouth. So, don't underestimate the power of it and your ability to grow an audience through that medium.

Also, when you come at it from the mindset of 'sharing', you're sharing your blog post, you're sharing your advice, you're sharing your offer, you're sharing the opportunity for you to make their life easier. I find that marketing is all about how we frame things in our own mind. If you're struggling with this then you must start reframing how you approach what you do.

- How can you share more?
- How can you give more?
- How can you help more?
- How can you connect more?

These are the questions that will drive your marketing behaviour and will change the game for how you put yourself out there.

I recently gave a little tip on Instagram stories that got shared so often it kind of surprised me. The tip was: share with people regularly, how they can work with you. We have followers who potentially want what we have – which is why they are following us, and we don't tell them the obvious thing of how we work, what's in it for them and what to do now.

Marketing isn't hard. Just remember that your mindset determines what you do. If you see the act of putting yourself out there as fun then it will be fun, if you see it as scary then that's what it will be – remember to have a trickster mindset and things will be SO much easier!

Change your mindset and you change the game.

To grab the free downloadable for this section on how you can BRAND BOLD, head to

www.playbigbrandbold.com/resources

It's your
CALL

—

"DON'T CHARGE YOUR 'WORTH' – YOU'RE PRICELESS"

Chapter Twelve

—

DARLING YOU'RE WORTH IT

f I had a dollar for every time I heard this phrase, I'd be a very rich woman! As I shared earlier, when I started my business and stepped out from behind someone else's brand, I wasn't charging anywhere near the amount of money I was charging for the same skills outside my business.

The sad thing is – it's common. And it's common with women whether they've come out of junior corporate roles or senior ones. I was speaking to a head of business recently who has gone out on her own and we were having this very conversation, and it honestly baffles me.

Why do we think what we do is worth so little?

Why do we think that people won't pay us what they've paid us in the past when we're basically doing the same work?

If you're looking for an answer here – I don't have one for you, sorry!

But what I can do is bring it to the surface so that we're more aware of it and hopefully can change that behaviour. The great thing is that once you get over it, then pricing confidence becomes your friend.

There's an interesting thing that happens when you become, as Brené Brown would say, dangerously confident. It basically means you've reached that place in life and business where you just don't care what others think. You feel comfortable in your own skin, you know your worth, you have something to say and you're not afraid to say it.

Now don't get me wrong – I'm not there every day, but some days I am and it's such a freeing place to be. I always remind my students and community – confidence comes from the small steps of courage we take every day – someone else said that by the way, I just don't know who, but I bloody love it!

So, let's talk money, shall we?

Ooowww did I just feel an intake of air? Did your butt clench just a little? Haha – I get it. This is a super uncomfortable conversation for some people. There's the whole 'I'm not worth it, we shouldn't talk about money, it's vulgar; I'm embarrassed to talk about it' and all the rest. But the more you get used to talking about and looking at the money in your business the better you'll be at making more.

Remember, what you focus on expands. And no, that's not the only thing you'll be focusing on, but it helps to know what's going on.

Now, pricing is a topic I enjoy talking about with clients. If you want to position your business as a premium solution, you must position yourself and your pricing and packages in that way too.

There are two key things I think you need to know and think about with this topic. One is that people want to pay for an outcome. They aren't looking to just pay you for what you do in a specific moment, they aren't paying just for the skills you have and the time it takes, they are paying you to take care of a problem for them, and that's what you need to sell.

What many of us think is – who will pay for my services? I think – who will pay for my solution, who wants to play bigger, who wants to package so it works for their customers, who wants to love their brand?

So, it's time to reframe. Who wants to feel amazing and healthy? Who wants to run incredible events? Who wants to have a website that people love to read and connect with? Who wants to have a PR professional on their team spruiking their wares? Those are the questions you want to ask because you're focusing on the solution. Remember, people pay you to take care of a problem they have.

Creating packages that solve your client's problems means you can charge more for the outcome you provide and the problem you solve. Saying that, you need to think about what those needs, problems and pain points are so you can speak to those. You'll also have to dig into what those things are in your business that you offer your clients that aren't hourly or commodity based.

Now I've been a money student for a long time, and between the likes of Denise Duffield-Thomas, Bill Baron, Tony Robbins and Sara Blakely, just to name a few, there are premium money mindsets I think can make a huge difference to how you price your services in your business.

MONEY MINDSET #1
YOU ATTRACT WHAT YOU BELIEVE

As they say – you attract what you put out. So, if you feel like it's hard to make money, it's hard to attract clients, you wouldn't pay for X, Y or Z, then often you'll attract those types of people. If you believe that your time is only worth the hourly rate that you're charging, then that's what you'll get back.

There are people who charge at the high end and people who charge at the low end for similar things. What is the difference? Is it their skill, or is it how they value what they do and the solution they provide? If you're not willing to invest in yourself for the things that matter to you, you might attract clients who feel the same way and aren't willing to invest in your premium packages or products.

The other belief to master here is the belief that your clients can get what they want and need from you. If you don't believe that you have the answer and you can solve their problem, that will come through when you're talking to them. You must believe and know that what you have is the answer to someone's problem. Even if the client is unsure if you know you can fix it, do it, achieve it, deliver it – then your belief in yourself and confidence you can help them can be enough for both of you.

So, in mindset one – you need to strengthen your internal belief that you can have what you want and you can deliver what others need. If you can achieve that, then

1) you will attract clients who believe it as well and believe you can solve their problem, and

2) your clients will see and feel that confidence in the solution even though they may not believe themselves just yet – but they are willing to take the chance on you.

Confidence is so important in business because it comes across when you're sharing what you have and when you're speaking to people. If you seem unsure then it's harder for the person your speaking to to believe you can help.

MONEY MINDSET #2
YOUR PREMIUM PRICES ARE NOT A REFLECTION OF WHO YOU ARE

Run your business like a business and not like a self-validation tool.

What does that mean?

Well, it fits into mindset #2 – You are not your business. Your successes or failures are not you; your pricing is not you.

You offer a result, a service and hopefully a transformation for your clients. You are selling a solution – you are not selling yourself.

Your personal worth or value does not change. The marketable value of what you offer – your products and service – does.

So, I want to say that again – your value does not change. The marketable value of what you offer does.

This is big for many women. So often we say, my value is based on how well my business does or if that client says yes or no. You have to move that belief. This is where the trickster comes in as well, if this is something that you suffer with. This is where trying and testing, seeing what happens and having a bit of fun with what you do helps you disconnect from your value versus what you offer in your business. So, if you try something and it bombs (which has happened to me), it's not personal. Just try something different. It's only been through the iterations of my products and services that I've found exactly what works for me and my clients, but that doesn't mean everything has succeeded. I wish, but that's not how it works.

The fees you charge are not what you're worth; it's the value you bring to someone. Also, taking your worth out of the equation means you're charging a commercial value on the skills and products and services you deliver. It's not about how much someone will pay for you, it's what they will pay for this 'thing' you have. Always remember that there is a paper clip at Tiffany's for $180. #justsaying

Pricing is a strategy – that's it. It's like brand positioning. It sets you at a certain level regarding what you deliver to your client. Your pricing tells a story to your customers about what you do and how you help, but it's not a reflection of you as a person.

There are a lot of things I've underpriced on purpose in my business because they have been an attraction tool to a bigger offering.

MONEY MINDSET #3
PRICING AND PACKAGING WITH HIGHER PRICES ARE NOT ABOUT CHARGING A LOT, IT'S ABOUT CREATING AS MUCH VALUE AS YOU CAN

A lot of times when we talk about charging more we think, *well, I can't do that, that's just greedy*. Once again, a limiting mindset. If I work with a client to get them confident to put themselves out there, charge more, provide more value to their clients and help them get out of their head and get their business, product or service out into the world, what is that worth?

If you can show the value you provide to your clients – and think about the things that your clients say to you – then solving that problem for someone means that you'll have some people who will pay $10 for it or $10,000 for it. It depends on what the value of solving that problem is for them. When you come from a place of adding value and solving a problem you can charge whatever resonates for you, and if you position your business at that level then you'll attract clients who are happy to pay that.

My clients say that I've reduced their stress about their business, they have way more clarity of what they're doing, they are charging more and giving their clients more, they feel more confident and more connected to their work and the outcomes.

The other way you can look at this is how can you create so much value that the investment they have put in is a fraction of the outcome they get.

MONEY MINDSET #4
PREMIUM MEANS INVESTING, NOT SPENDING

This was a big shift for me a few years ago. I was thinking, *Wow will people 'spend' that much money? How much do they 'spend' on other things?*

I look at courses or training I do and after I apply the things I've learnt,

I look at the tangible impact it's had on my business. To give you an example, I went along to a conference. Tony Robbins was one of the speakers but there were a whole lot of other speakers there too. I had been looking for a 'selling from the stage' course for about two years at this point, and on that day a guy named Andy Harrington got up to speak. He was dynamic, energised and an amazing storyteller. He was also selling a four-day course called Public Speakers University.

Now, to anyone else in the room who wasn't interested in this topic or training – he would have come across as salesy and annoying (those were the words of my virtual assistant who was there with me on the day), but to me (his ideal client) it was music to my ears. I knew that similar courses were going for $5k plus, but for the four days it would be around $3999. Now once again, to someone else that amount of money was crazy – but to me, it was a bargain and it was what I was looking for. Remember one woman's trash is another woman's treasure. I did the course, which besides my master's was the biggest investment that I've made in myself in a single purchase. But by using what I learnt in that four-day training, I've created one of the key income streams in my business, which has been worth a lot more than the $4,000 and will continue to help me grow my business in the way I want to.

I'm glad I invested in that training, and when I'm focused on what I spend my money on, I'm excited to spend it or – let's reframe it – 'invest' in myself because I know the benefits I'll be getting from it. Your clients are the same. They see the investment and the solution to their problems. So, you're not here to talk to everyone – you're here to talk to those who want what you have.

We set our prices and packages and then someone says you're too expensive, and all our insecurities come up. But remember – if that is how they feel then THEY ARE NOT YOUR PERSON. They are not the client you're looking to attract.

When you can change your own mindset around your pricing and packaging – that your clients are investing in what they need – the amount you charge will become easier to detach your personal worth from.

MONEY MINDSET #5
LESS EQUALS MORE

What's the big dream? Ask yourself that question. For most people I work with or speak to, it's to run a business they love, doing the thing they want, but not working all the hours that god sends so they can have some balance.

So, what's the only way to do that?

Charge more to fewer clients so that you're making the money you want but not killing yourself in the process.

We ideally want to move away from hourly based charging as a whole – or what I call transaction charging – to transformational packaging. Now if you're sitting there thinking, *Suzanne, but my industry charges by the hour, that's what we do,* then this is where your mindset might need to change around where you position yourself. If you've only ever charged hourly then you most likely have only ever attracted clients that want to pay that way. When you package what you do, you'll attract clients looking for a solution rather than just a pair of hands to complete a task.

The ideal outcome is to become known as an expert in your field for what you do. So, the key here is to focus on your core message and the services that deliver to those core messages. If you feel overwhelmed with all of your social media channels, then just focus on one and kill it in that platform. If you have too many products and services, then just focus on one or two and drive that home. If you want to build wealth in your business then focus on the packages you can deliver, the transformation you can achieve and work on those things.

Nail the problem, package, price, and promotion, and you'll be attracting clients who want what you have at the price you want to charge.

—

Chapter Thirteen

IT'S ALL ABOUT MOMENTUM

've learnt a lot over the last few years and hopefully it means that you don't have to make the same mistakes or take as long as I did to clue in to some of the things I really should have been doing from the beginning that would have made all the difference.

STRATEGIES FOR BUILDING MOMENTUM

1. IDENTIFY WHAT MAKES YOU UNIQUE AND DIFFERENT

If you want to stand out, then you must know what you do differently. This could be a particular way you work, it could be your branding, it could be the take on your message, it could be how easy it is for people to work with you – so ease of use. It doesn't have to be mind-blowing, but ideally, you'll know why you're different or how you work with your clients in your own unique way.

I work with large corporates and with small businesses and have built businesses across both playing fields, I know how to price and package and brand and create core messages for both types of businesses. It gives me breadth and depth that a lot of other coaches in my space don't have – or if they do, they don't use that as their differentiator.

Think about the different clients that you've worked with, what you like to do and how you like to do it. Do you have a unique mix of things you do for clients? Maybe the way you talk about how you help them has a different angle? If you can find your unique look, feel, message or target audience, then for marketing – or, as I prefer to call it, 'sharing' – what you have, you and/or your business will become someone that people think about when they think about what you do.

2. CREATE STRATEGIC RELATIONSHIPS

Connect with people with similar audiences to yours but who do different things. Don't worry about the competition; position yourself as a thought leader and a leader in your industry, and people will gravitate to you. So, write down at least three people you could strategically align with. This means you build a relationship where you support each other. This may mean referring work, co-advertising to each other's audience, running workshops or events together, reposting each other's content, etc. If you can build up two or three great partnerships, it can go a long way to help you build momentum in your business, because you're accessing more audiences that are your target audience.

There are two things I will say regarding strategic relationships – first, find someone you can trust, you like and you get along with because it is a two-way street, and the second thing is that if you're not sure, then ask around about who has a similar audience but does something different, and then have a chat with them and start building relationships. The one thing that has to be consistent is your brand alignment. Find people who have similar values to you otherwise you'll jar your audience, which is not what you want to do.

3. WORK OUT A CONTENT AND MARKETING PLAN

People make this a lot more complicated than it needs to be. Anyone who has any serious kudos, impact, or brand usually has a consistent content strategy where you're seeing a lot of what they put out regularly.

There are a few entrepreneurs I follow who I either get an email from on a Thursday or their video comes out on a Tuesday. The *Brand Builder's Lab* podcast comes out every Thursday now, and I send an email on the Thursday afternoon or Friday morning. Give your audience a window of consistency so that they know when you're going to be connecting with them.

It's easy to get into the rhythm if you commit to it. Batching is one way to help you deliver this, and one of my big goals is to record at least four podcasts at any one time so that I don't have to scramble each week. Sometimes it works, sometimes it doesn't. But trying is the key!

When I work with clients, one of the things we work on is 'less is more'. When you have a piece of content – old or new, then it's about repurposing it so you write something once and then you may get 5–10 different posts out of it.

Say you write a blog post – you have it on your website, post it to Twitter (evergreen), Instagram a pic of it, share to your Facebook business page, then to groups, pin it on Pinterest, post it as an article on LinkedIn (not just sharing the link) and then maybe you do a Facebook Live about it. If you're regularly creating written or video content, then build momentum like that.

Now, even if you have a roaring business – continuing to evaluate the response you're getting and how you're engaging with your audience is key. So keep building.

If you're starting out and you get discouraged because you don't think people are reading what you're writing or you're not getting engagement on it – it takes time. Nothing happens overnight, so persistence is your best friend!

4. FIND A ROUTINE

One of the questions I am asked fairly often is 'How do you plan your week?'

The follow-up to that question, 'I just don't know what I'm supposed to be doing'.

When you're in a job, you know the tasks, projects, outputs that are required of you. But when you go into your own business it's totally up to you what happens.

So, if you struggle with this, here is an overview of how I work, which you could use as a base to work out what works for you. Saying that – some people like structure and others don't.

On a Monday, Tuesday and Friday I'm focused on running the marketing, branding and projects for corporate clients. On a Wednesday or Thursday, I'm usually running presentation training sessions for clients, doing a brand strategy session or speaking at an event. No matter what else I'm doing on a Thursday, Thursdays are my finance days. I check my accounting software Xero, I chase up invoices, send out proposals, check the bank balance etc. I also follow up proposals that I've sent out if I haven't heard back.

This is what I like to call 'running my business like a business'. I'm not only the talent, but I'm the web developer, social media manager, accounts and sales department and you need all of those things in order for your business to run well. So I make time for those things.

I outsource a lot as well. I have a VA; I recently hired someone to sort out the SEO on my website; I have an accountant who does my BAS and tax return. But that still leaves me with a lot to do. The good thing is that if you get into the habit of running your business efficiently and you give yourself the space and time to work on your business and not just in it, then you'll start to see the momentum rise.

The other thing that has worked very well for me is time blocking. The time I book for myself is non-negotiable.

I don't change it for clients, I don't keep moving it around – I respect my own time and do the work I've booked in. Once again, when you start doing this consistently, you'll also gain momentum because you're operating like a business, doing the things you know you need to do and gaining traction through regular and consistent execution.

5. FOCUS ON SALES AND BUSINESS-BUILDING ACTIVITIES

I want to ask you a big question: Is what you're doing at the moment in your business giving you the return and clients you want?

If it's not, then focusing your time and effort on getting super clear on your message as well as storyselling and marketing is where you need to be.

Having your pricing, packaging, and easy access to what you do and then making the offer is what it's all about. If you don't make the offer, people can't take you up on it! I know this can be hard for some people but learning to make the offer and promote your business will obviously make all the difference. So do the things that matter. Think about what has made you successful before or what other people do to be successful and do those things. Don't pussyfoot around. Do things that matter and make a difference on a day-to-day basis. Remember, it's all the little things that count and if you do those enough, there will be a tipping point and let me tell you – you will see it in a big way.

6. STICK WITH THE ONE THING

I recently did a podcast interview on the *Brand Builder's Lab* podcast with Jamie Palmer from Outlier Marketing Group in the US (episode 65). We discussed 'shiny object syndrome' that so many entrepreneurs have because we're creative beings. Jamie talked about the importance of sticking with the one thing and optimising it. And when you feel like you want to get creative, instead of abandoning the course, program or thing you've worked so hard to build, get creative with your marketing instead.

I can't tell you how much I love this, and I wish I had focused on it much sooner in my business. When I think about really big, successful online businesses, most of them have been doing the same thing for years. They haven't been chopping and changing and trying new and different things every year – they keep building on what they have. This has meant momentum and success.

I have to be honest, this took me too long to get. I hope it doesn't take you too long. I had all the things. Events, workshops, a membership, big courses, little courses, strategy session, corporate training, speaking. I'm not even kidding. I had all that running at once and eventually after really stepping back and looking at what I was doing, what was working and what wasn't I saw I couldn't make any one thing super successful with so many things on the go. So, I made the decision to just focus on three things; my one signature course, Brand Builder's Academy; being a paid speaker; and running presentation skills training with teams and individuals.

The relief has been pretty epic. To focus all my energy, marketing, money and focus into those things quickly saw a huge increase in highly paid private and corporate gigs that outweighed the revenue I had made in previous months with the multiple products and services.

I can't stress this to you enough. When you narrow your focus and put everything into just those one or two things, you'll see them grow exponentially and you'll wish you'd done it sooner. I sure wish I had.

7. GO HARD OR GO HOME

If you're here to build a business, then focus on what it takes to build your business and keep moving forward. Don't give up after two months because you're not internet famous. Build with integrity, patience, clarity and purpose and chip away at what you want in a way that feels right for you.

Once again, it's about getting your head in the game and doing the things you need to do to operate your business – not your hobby, but your business – in the right way. That means products and services that work, the right systems to make your life easy and the courage to put yourself out there to attract the right people you want to work with.

Showing up every day isn't easy, and I show up more on some days than others, because I'm human. You have to find the right energy level and balance for you and your business but as one of my gorgeous clients once said, "My desire for success is greater than my fear of failure." And I really hope you adopt that for yourself as well.

Chapter Fourteen

CREATE YOUR OWN DAMN OPPORTUNITIES

Okay, so I'm going to go out on a limb here and say that sometimes we expect things just to happen for us. We look at that other woman and say, "She's so lucky, things just happen for her. Opportunities just come for her. Why doesn't that happen to me?"

Whaa Whaa…

Yes, I just said Whaa Whaa – you heard me right!

Very few people in life are lucky. There are so many people who have succeeded who started with nothing. They worked their butts off and created their own opportunities and that's what you need to start doing if you're not doing it already!

So, you're sitting there thinking… *Well Suz, how can I create more opportunities for myself?*

It's up to us to make things happen. No one else will do it for you, so you must be brave and clear and focused on what you want and how you will go about getting it.

Opportunities are like cars. Bear with me. ☺

If you haven't listened to my video 'The Practical Girls Guide to

Manifestation', this is the general gist. When you're looking to buy a car, you start by browsing either online or heading to car dealers to look at ones that you think you want. You may see a model you didn't even know existed and then suddenly, you see that make and model everywhere. Everyone has that same car that you've been looking to buy. How had you not noticed this before?

Well, this happens because you're subconsciously looking for it. You're now aware of that car, make and model so your brain is searching for it because it's front and centre for you. It's something that you think you want and so you're looking for reassurance and signs that it's the right car for you.

The same goes for opportunities you want. Actually knowing what you want will mean that your subconscious scans for those opportunities. So, you may have had opportunities in the past, but you weren't looking for them, so you missed the boat, but now that you know how it works, you can start programming yourself to see those opportunities when they come along. That's why setting intentions at the beginning of each week is a great practise. I used to think it was a bit woo woo, but when I researched more about how our brain connects with the things we really want and searches for them, I was sold.

If at the beginning of the week I set the intention that this week I would like to secure two new clients, then it's not to say it's going to happen, but it's more likely to happen because I'm now looking for ways, either consciously or unconsciously, of how I can achieve that. Is there someone I need to follow up on, is there someone who has shown interest in what I do and wants to chat, is there a collaboration opportunity or a strategic partnership I could put into action? Your brain will start working in ways it hasn't before, and you'll see opportunities you haven't seen before.

As a follow on to setting intentions to create opportunities – the key is to not wait around for others to give you opportunities either. If there is an opportunity you see or that you think someone can give you, then ask. You know I ask for what I want all the time and if someone says no then I just move on. It's a bit of a game. I don't put all my eggs in one basket around my self-worth if someone says no. The more people I ask for things, the more noes I'll probably get. But the more yeses I'll get as well, compared to if I had never asked.

When it comes to your mindset around asking, I love how Elizabeth Gilbert talks about this in her book *Big Magic*. She talks about the two schools of thought when creating – the Martyrs and the Tricksters. So you can have the mindset of a martyr, which is 'I will do this even if it kills me, I take everything very seriously, it has to be painful to create and put yourself out there and it may cost me everything and that's how it can feel.' Whereas the trickster says, 'pick a card, any card – take a chance, let's have a little fun'. The trickster is looking at how to do things more playfully. She wants to put something out there and see what happens. Put it out there again and see what happens. If putting yourself out there feels hard or scary – then ask yourself why. Usually it's because we hang so much importance or seriousness on what we're doing. It's not that what you're doing isn't important but if you want to shift yourself into action, then you must change how you think about the things you do.

Wouldn't you like creating to be more fun? Wouldn't you like to feel more ease with the things you do? Have you been holding back from doing certain things in your business because of what you think it will take?

When it comes to creating your own opportunities around getting more clients there are a few things you can do to help yourself out.

The first thing is to literally ask people to refer you. I'm sure you have people around you who want to see you succeed and want to support you. Letting them know what you need and what you do specifically can make a big difference to how people show up for you.

I've said this before, you think people around you know what you do. But often they aren't thinking about you, they're thinking about themselves. So it's key to keep reminding them. Let them know what kind of people you're looking to connect with and get them thinking. If someone asks me directly to think of who I know then I'll do that!

If you're looking to get speaking gigs, then you've got a couple of options – either run your own events or connect with people who run events, understand what they are looking for and then ask! Once again, if they say no then it may be for a multitude of reasons. I've had people ask me if they can speak but I've either had a similar speaker before so it's not needed, or they may not be right for my audience. But usually I'll let them know. Remember that getting used to asking for what you want and being okay with no will give you more opportunities in the end.

Getting on podcasts is another way of playing bigger. Most podcasters will have a policy on their website outlining how they engage with guests and what you can do if you want to be a guest. The same goes for guest blogging. Most sites who take guest blogs have it outlined exactly what you need to do.

Once again, if you know what you want to do then you can look at ways to make that happen for yourself. Researching, being proactive, networking, and approaching people is all part of creating those opportunities for yourself. People talk as well. So, if you've been connecting with one person about something specific, you never know who they know who could be looking for someone like you.

As I always say – LISTENING WILL GET YOU MORE CLIENTS THAN TALKING WILL!

So, write down what your clients or community have been talking about or asking about. This is gold. It can give you content for months and help create the right products and services to sell to your audience. When you listen to your audience, what you create will be for them. When you create things like this, then it doesn't matter what anyone else has done before because it's how you do it and who you are and what you stand for that they are buying into.

So, when it comes to creating your own opportunities, get proactive, focus on what you want, seek those opportunities out and create a trickster mindset. It will help you put yourself out there more, with more ease, more fun, and less anguish than if you hold tight to your fear.

Step

U P

___

Chapter Fifteen

TOUGH LOVE

I recently recorded a podcast episode that had such an amazing response and reflects how I feel about business and where we are right now. It's the things I think you must know, the things you must think about, and it's about how you need to show up if you want to actually make your business work long term.

If you're reading this book and would prefer to listen to the audio for this podcast, then head to **www.suzchadwick.com/pod54** and dive in. Here is the transcript:

This week I'm doing something a little bit different and in all honesty, it's really just me giving a bit of a reality check to anybody out there who has just started a business or they've been in business for a little while and they are thinking that maybe they should just give up. Or, you've just started a business and you're wondering why you haven't already made six figures in the first 12 weeks of starting. So I hope that this is helpful, but it is a pep talk and it is something that I am really passionate about talking about.

Today I'm going to be talking about what it takes to get clients, how long it can take to build your business, what it takes to be successful, how you need to show up, why you need to get rid of the excuses, and why self-awareness and grit is everything in business.

Let's start with what it takes to get clients. Now, because I'm a business coach, I have had a lot of people come to me over the last couple of years and say, "I want to make 100 grand in the next six to twelve months." Now, just a little side note, they've got no audience, they've not had a business before, they currently have no following, they're not exactly clear on their products and services, and there is no message around why what they do is important, how it impacts the people that they're looking to serve, and what the offering is as well.

When it comes to getting clients, it's really important that you understand a couple of things. Number one, it takes time. It's not just going to happen overnight. Now, if you do something, if you have specific expertise and you already have people that want to work with you, then you can get clients pretty quickly, because you've actually started your business based on specific demand. And I'll give you an example of that. It took me time to get clients, but when I started, I already had women that I was working with who had friends that were like, "You have to work with this person, too." So I created an offering, very quickly, that was in direct need to the demand that I had been given already.

Whilst I didn't have a lot of clients to start with, that's where I got my first couple of clients from. And then it was through those interactions that I started to:

Build a little bit of an audience

Get referrals, because they knew other people

I got really clear on what it was that I wanted to be known for and what it was that I wanted to offer.

The other thing around that is it has evolved and changed over the last four to five years, which is how long I have had The Connection Exchange, how long I've been business coaching, et cetera. The second thing is, you have to show up every day and start connecting with people. Now the way that business is right now, we've got a lot of choices. There are a lot of people out there that may do similar things, and so it's really up to us to think about how we show up and how we connect with people.

If you think about the people that you've hired to do things for you, what was the process that you went through? Did you just kind of find them and immediately buy from them, or just hop on to their Instagram and think, "Yeah, okay, cool, I'm going to hire them to do whatever." Now, when it comes to a product-based business, if you're looking for a candle, then you might just purchase a candle that you find online through a business. If it's clothing, then you might see something you like and purchase it.

But if you are a service-based business, in reality, there are very few times where somebody's just going to find you and hire you without building some sort of awareness of you and trust. So my guess is that the people that you hired in a service-based way, that was not a small amount of money, is that you found them, you started following them, and then you decided to check them out even more, so you went to their website, you learned more about them, maybe you checked out their testimonials. You wanted to get to know them, and I'm sure their message really resonated for you if you decided to hire them.

Now, maybe you looked at potentially how you could work with them, and then you purchased from them. And that's how most businesses work. So, unless you've got something completely different to what other people offer, then you have to understand that you've got to show up and start connecting with people. And there really is no shortcut to that. There is no shortcut to building relationships. There's no shortcut to building trust. Unless you've got other people with really large followings who are singing your praises and referring you constantly, that really is just one of the channels that you can get business from. You've obviously got to do your own work and show up on your own channels to build that trust with the people that are following you.

The second thing is, what does it take to be successful? So, having a really clear idea for now of what you want to do, and I'm saying for now because it will change, you know, what you want to offer, what the benefit is to your *audience. If you haven't spoken with a whole bunch of people who are your potential clients or the people that you're targeting, then I'm going to ask you, "Why not?"*

You have to know your audience and what their pain points are, and what they want, and what they want to be in the world, and what they want to do, and what they want to have. You have to get under the skin of your audience. You've got to share your story, your vulnerabilities as well as your knowledge and your strengths. So you know what you're an expert in, and what you can help them to do.

You need to understand that nothing comes quickly. All of the people you see who are successful and who have waitlists or sold-out programmes or are filling stadiums and all the rest of it, they have been in business for 10 years, they have worked year-on-year to build what they have. They're the ones that keep showing up and doing the work and growing their audience, even when it's hard. Even when nobody is responding. Even when they're not selling anything. Because they understand that it's a long game and that you don't just show up and all of a sudden everything works.

Even people who you think have all of a sudden come out of nowhere and just started. They have all said that they tried different things. They had different iterations of their business. Different iterations of their products. And they're still crafting it and honing it and building it. It really takes that time for you to understand what works. The other thing with that is the market changes all the time, so you have to learn to pivot quickly.

So what do you need to do? Well, the first thing is, you need to be tenacious, patient and driven. If you don't want to hustle, that's fine. For me, when I talk about hustling, it means that I've got a really clear goal of what I want to do and I do everything in my power to achieve that goal. That's what hustling is for me. I know that hustling's had a really bad sort of rep, and you can use whatever word works for you. Tenacity is a good one. It is seeing the goal and going after it and making sure that you are leaving no stone unturned. That you are doing everything that you need to do. And that you have made a decision to do the things that are uncomfortable. Not only that, but that you're willing to learn to move quickly and be really agile in your business. So, read the market. Try different things. See what you enjoy, what works, what sells, and then learn and pivot from there.

Things I have loved have flopped, and things I have not enjoyed as much have done really well. I feel like after five years in business I've finally settled in to having the products and services that I love and that are really profitable and serve my audience really well, but it's only because I really dove in to knowing my audience and asking them lots of questions, and really understanding that these two or three people who are in my community and who buy everything that I create, they are my ideal client. They are the ones who I create things for because they're the ones I want to serve.

And so, the things that I create really resonate for them, so I use them as my baseline, and when I'm thinking about doing something new, they are the people I go to because I want a million of them. I want a million women in business who are like them, who want the things that I have.

You have to understand that you have got to learn as you go as well, and all of the products and services I have right now, they support what I want to be known for. Some of them have been around for a few years. Brand Builders Academy started two years ago, we're in year three now. And the workshops that I've done, I've done different iterations of them and I feel like I've really settled into those now and I love them and they deliver exactly what I want them to, to my audience, but there have been a lot of things that I've tried that haven't worked. So if you think that you'll just nail it first time round, then I'm here to tell you that that seldom happens.

But I want you to be okay with that. I think what happens a lot of the time is that we try things and they aren't as successful as we want them to be, or we don't value the three people that signed up, or the one person that showed up, or the 10 people that decided to come along and buy. We think that that's a failure because we see all of these people who have got millions or hundreds of thousands or thousands of followers. We think that if we don't have the same level of success immediately that it wasn't worth it and wasn't successful. That we didn't win in that instance.

It's just so important to understand that you have to grow your business. It's like a plant. You plant the seed, you water it, you tend to it, you give it attention, you give it love, and it grows over time. Your business is literally like a tree. Does a big, amazing tree grow in three months? If you're ever thinking about why is this not happening faster for me, I just want you to really understand that that's what it takes, and that you may have some real success at different times, but it's something that you've got to keep at on a regular basis. And in order to do that, the next point is you've got to get rid of the excuses.

If you're sitting here and got a whole lot of excuses popping up in your head, then I am calling you on that. You either want this or you don't. I share a story on my sales page in a video where there was a moment a few years ago where I had to call myself out on my own behaviour, and I had to make the decision to show up and do the things that are uncomfortable.

I had to know what was uncomfortable for me and then decide, "How bad do I want this?" Was I going to show up more? Was I going to recognise that I wanted to be a leader in my field, and not be embarrassed to claim that space and be bold about it? Was I going to choose to play big and was I going to choose to brand bold? And was I going to encourage and support other women to do the same?

We have excuses so that we feel safe and stay playing small. We have excuses to give ourselves a knock out. We have excuses that we don't have to do the things that we find hard. And if you're not willing to do the things that are hard, uncomfortable, or that stretch you, then business may not be for you, because I don't know a single person in business who doesn't struggle with the reality of doing the hard stuff.

I know that being a business owner has totally been glorified that it's glamorous and it's amazing, and there are moments that it is amazing, otherwise we wouldn't do what we do. But I think that there is... I don't know what it is, it's a lack of reality around how hard it is and what you have to go through to get to *the glamorous stuff, and what you have to go through to be successful.*

Did you think that it was going to be easy? I guess that's my question. Maybe you did. Maybe because you look at what other people do and you think, "Well, if they can do it, I can do it." And you can. But I just think that there are definitely things happening in the business world where people just think that, "Tomorrow I'll be successful and I'll get a client and it'll be awesome and I'll be done." And that's just not how it is.

So, the next thing I wanted to talk about was self-awareness. One thing I see a lot is a lack of self-awareness and honesty. There are the excuses but there is either a choice to be blind to what you need to work on yourself, or there is a genuine lack of self-awareness. When I talk about self-awareness, it's recognising what you're really good at and recognising what you need to move, learn, grow, change or shift as well. That self-awareness means you can get the help you need where you need it, and that you can recognise when you're a barrier. That means, you are a barrier to your own success. But the great thing is that if you know it and you see it, then you can change it.

Self-awareness is also about being realistic when it comes to what it takes and what you're willing to do. So, could I be doing more in my business? Yes is the answer. Am I working as hard as I could? No is the answer. So this is me reflecting on myself. I watch TV every night, I am addicted to Billions, I choose not to work on weekends. There are just boundaries that I put in place for myself but when I started my business, for the first two years, I worked night and day, weekends as well, and I was working a full-time job, so I did what I had to do to get things off the ground and make it happen. It was hard, but I made a conscious decision that this is what I wanted and this was going to be the work that I wanted to do, and I was going to do everything in my power to make it a success.

And at the end of the day, that's what I did. I did not stop when it got hard, I did not stop when it took so much longer than I thought it was going to, and eventually I went part-time and I still work a couple of days in my corporate job because I love it and I enjoy it and I run that branding division.

But those are the decisions that I've made for myself, and you have to make the decisions that are right for you. And I say this all the time.

One of my friends who has got an amazing tech start-up and she's doing awesome and is on, you know, the best '30 under 30' hot lists for entrepreneurs and all the rest of it. She continued to be a barista part-time whilst she was building her business in order to do what she had to do to make it a success. I think a lot of times we think that if we just throw it all in and do what we have to do, that it will work. And sometimes it will, but you have to decide, what else am I willing to do to make this work?

And there's no simple answer for that. That is a decision you have to make yourself. But at the end of the day what it comes down to is grit, and grit is everything. Google says, "Grit is the persistence and perseverance and passion to achieve long-term goals." Sometimes you will hear grit referred to as mental toughness.

Angela Duckworth, a researcher at the University of Pennsylvania, suggests that grit is a strong predictor of success and ability to reach one's goals. And so grit is exactly what it says on the tin. So, my question to you is, how bad do you want this? If I said it was going to take two years to get your business off the ground, would you still do it? If I said it was going to take five years, would you still do it? If I said you'll only reach what you really want for your business in the next 10 years, would you do it?

What would you do to make it happen? What would you take on to make it happen? What would you change to make it happen? Or would you decide that that's too long, and too hard, and so you're just not going to do it and you're going to throw it in? Once again, everybody who is anybody who has been successful, has said it took way longer than they thought it would. But they stuck in there and they did what they had to do to make it happen.

So my question is, do you have the grit to make this work? Are you willing to get uncomfortable and persevere and do you have the passion to achieve your long-term goals? How big is your vision? They talk about your "why", but I think about it as my vision. My vision is to serve more women globally to help them *Play Big* and *Brand Bold*. To help them to love to learn to market their business and to share what it is they've got to say, and for them to step up, to be leaders in their field. That is my big vision.

That is what I hold close to and tight to, every day, when I send audio DMs to clients and I say, "You have got to step up and you have got to choose to be a leader." That is why I do what I do. When I say to somebody, "I have to be honest with you. I don't see you showing up so you can't complain that your business is not going where you want it to go if you're not willing to do the work that has to be done."

How serious are you about this business, or are you just wanting to "play at it", and I'm doing that in inverted commas, because you thought that you'd make six figures in 12 months. Do you have the mental toughness and tenacity to stick with this? Are you willing to find the confidence through all those small acts of courage to achieve what you want? And are you going to fold when it gets too hard because you didn't reach the goals you wanted in the first 10 weeks?

So I'm just going to say, it is time to woman-up and make the decision. I am nowhere near where I thought I would be by now. I'm in a good place and I love my business and I love what I'm doing, but there is so much that I still haven't done. But I can guarantee you that I am not going anywhere even if it takes another 10 years, because I am not going to look back on my dream and my big goals and desires and say, "I didn't have enough grit and determination, and I didn't have enough self-awareness to really see where I needed to change and evolve."

And so, I am giving you this pep talk and sharing this with you because I want you to dig in, and I want you to decide how bad you want this, and I want you to stop putting all of these limitations on yourself about what you think it should be. It is time to decide to be a leader in your field. It is time to show your face. It is time to step up and do the things that you find uncomfortable and do it every single day. And if you're not willing to do it, then you've got to decide whether you really want this or not. But the big question I want you to ask yourself is, if you don't do it, what are you going to regret?

So, that is this week's bonus episode. It's a little bit of tough love, but it's done with a whole lot of love. Because I want big things for you, and I want you to get out of your own way, and I want you to feel excited about the achievements that you're making and the difference that you're making in the lives of your clients. And these things that you are doing that you never thought in a million years you would do, that you have 100% got it in you to do it.

I want you to know that I am cheering for you, and the women who follow you are cheering for you, and the people who love you are cheering for you.

Chapter Sixteen

HIRING YOURSELF AS THE CEO OF YOUR BUSINESS

Now if you haven't worked out already, this book is about challenging you to step up, stand out and make the decision to be all in. If you are all in there is one more thing you need to make sure you've done – or that you do – and that's hiring yourself TODAY as the CEO of your business.

So many times I think we treat ourselves as the employee of our business and we're waiting for someone else to work out the business, branding and marketing strategy. We're waiting for someone else to look after the finances and figure out how we're going to grow. We work in our business like an employee and think that somehow growing our business will miraculously happen without us doing anything. I kinda call that 'putting your head in the sand'. But what I want you to realise (if you don't know it already) is that nothing will happen if you don't make it happen. Nothing will happen if you don't step up, take the reins and start to call the shots. If you decide to hire yourself as the CEO and step into that role, your business will grow and things will start to shift and change. And you wanna know something else that's really cool about doing this? You get to give your employee a pay rise! Yep you... you get a pay rise because you're doing the work that matters and actually steering the ship, making decisions, getting clear on what you're aiming for and how you're growing your biz.

Most the business owners I've worked with or spoken to share a similar story in one version or another. They really saw their business grow when they decided to make the time to plan, focus on what they really want and create a structure, strategy and systems to scale.

That work is the work of a CEO. That work is the work of someone taking the time to evaluate what is happening in the business and what needs to happen in the future. Look at where you are now and where you want to be and figure out the gap in between. Do you need to hire someone to help you work out your numbers and metrics, or is it something you can learn? Are you running financial reports regularly or do you have no idea how much money you have coming in? Do you know where your clients and website traffic is coming from or is it a complete mystery?

Here are key activities to look at if you want to step up as the CEO in your business.

1. DRIVE THE BUSINESS TO BECOME A LEADER IN YOUR CATEGORY

What are you doing to become a leader in your field or category? Are you focused on becoming a thought leader, to build a connected brand, to stand out in your market? Is this something that you're thinking about? Is it something that you want?

If you're saying – well I don't want to be leader, my questions is, what do you think leader means? It doesn't mean you have to be the biggest. It doesn't mean that you have to speak on stages – it means that you are sought after and are known as one of the best.

Becoming a leader really means that you have decided to play a pivotal role in driving your business forward. It's having a clear brand strategy and understanding where you want to position yourself. What you want to be known for is a good place to start.

2. CREATE EFFECTIVE SALES AND MARKETING CHANNELS FOR YOUR BUSINESS

In the Brand Builder's Academy community, I talk about really stepping up and how you can do that. What activities are you consciously implementing based on your constant learning?

I was watching new marketing videos on YouTube the other day and I'm reading about four different branding and business books at the moment too. Now you don't need to do that – I just love learning. However, you do need to work out how you're going to teach yourself some things you may not know or that you want to get better at.

If you're telling yourself you're not good at sales and marketing or you don't like it, then you're going to struggle in your business. Because no matter what people say, there is always an element of sales and marketing. And yes, you build a brand and following who want what you have but just like I always say with Gorman – they have all that but they are still marketing to their customers so that we know what they have, when they have it and how we can get it.

3. LEADERSHIP OF OPERATIONS, SALES, MARKETING, ECOMMERCE/WEBSITE, EVENTS, FINANCE AND HR

This is your baseline. The operations are the workings of the business on a day-to-day basis. Do you have a clear idea of what you're working towards and what you're doing for your clients, AND also for your own business?

Do you have a plan or strategy for what you're working towards? Once again this is something I teach and go deeper into in BBA and I'm consistently trying to shift the perception that this is a big task. It's not a big task, but it's a focused task. It's a task that you learn how to do and becomes a skill you have forever.

4. DRIVE A 'CUSTOMER FIRST' MINDSET IN YOUR BUSINESS

How are you developing your customer experience? Understanding your customer's problem and then building a really solid customer experience solving that problem and creating an emotional connection can make the world of difference.

So how are you creating great customer experience? How are you solving your customer's problems?

My customers are women in business who want to step up as the CEO but they don't know how to. My customers are the women in business who want to learn how to create the right business structure, strategies and systems to scale. My customers are the action takers with the big dreams who want to succeed but also understand that they have to learn key business skills along the way. My customers are the ones who want to be bold and stand out with their unique voice.

So what are the experiences that I'm creating for them? Who your customer is, is not just a woman between the ages of 35-44 with a service-based business looking for a copywriter. Go deep into the desires they have for themselves, their business, their family – whatever it is for them.

What does having a customer first mindset look like for you?

5. TRANSFORM YOUR BUSINESS INTO A COMPELLING CONSUMER BRAND

What does 'compelling' really mean? The meaning according to Google is: evoking interest, attention, or admiration in a powerfully irresistible way. Not able to be refuted; inspiring conviction. Not able to be resisted.

So how are you evoking interest in what you do and how you do it?

How are you attracting attention and admiration for what you do?

Are you creating a powerfully irresistible product, service or brand?

Really thinking about these words and how you can do more of that is super important. I honestly think it's only when we spend the time to think more deeply about our customers and their problems that we can come up with compelling words, messaging, products and services that really speak to them.

What stories are you telling yourself? Take time to write them down. If you were to truly think about the key things you have to do in your business but you're not doing, then ask yourself why you're not doing them. Then ask yourself, what are the stories I'm telling myself when it comes to that task?

6. ENSURE THE BUSINESS' VALUES AND MISSION ARE UPHELD

We have discussed this earlier, but having your vision, mission and values being a living breathing thing in your business – that you look at and are connected to every day in your business – will guide you with your decisions.

7. ACCURATE AND TIMELY REPORTING

It's so important to provide yourself with accurate and timely reporting. My hubby – bless him – sends me a report every month on where my traffic is coming from, what's working and what's not. After listening to Karlie on the podcast in episode 66 we are now looking closely at broken links, time on site, bounce rate and site speed as some of our reporting metrics.

If I'm running paid ads, I look at the cost per lead and importantly, the conversion rate as you don't want to throw money away if things aren't working for you.

8. ARE YOU RUNNING YOUR FINANCIAL REPORTS EVERY MONTH OR QUARTER?

If you aren't, why not? Is it because you don't know how; you don't have the software; you can't be bothered?

Running your financial reports means you can work out how to change your strategy each year to increase your revenue. But if you don't know what's going on then that's a hard thing to do.

I set a financial goal at the beginning of each financial year and use that goal to drive my business decisions, brand and marketing strategy. It means I know how much I'll need to dedicate to my marketing budget if I'm looking to 10x it.

9. BUILD STRONG RELATIONSHIPS WITH KEY EXTERNAL STAKEHOLDERS INCLUDING CUSTOMERS AND SUPPLIERS

Who are you building relationships with? Working out who you can connect with, collaborate with and build relationships with in your business can be a key part of your growth strategy.

Who are you working with or bringing into the business to support you and run things for you, in order for you to stay in your zone of genius?

The great thing about this concept is when you decide to step into this role the benefits are pretty amazing:

- You grow your business with real purpose and focused effort
- By growing your business it allows you to give your employee (you) a pay rise
- You grow a global – or at the very least, really powerful – brand
- You feel the satisfaction of learning how to create strategies that work

It's time – I'm just going to call it. It's time to step up and start creating your own opportunities. It's time to start playing bigger and branding bolder, it's time to say – yep, I'm going to do it and get profesh!

So if you haven't hired yourself as the CEO of your biz yet – maybe it's time to put out a 'I'm hiring' ad and then apply for it yourself!

Trust me, it'll be the best hire you ever make!

Chapter Seventeen

WHEN ALL IS SAID AND DONE

After all is said and done, I can't believe I'm writing this little thanks to you, my amazing reader. Thanks for choosing to show up, step up and stand out. Thanks for getting this far and diving into this book and hanging out. I bet you have loads of things you could be doing right now, but you've chosen to spend this time with me.

I really hope that this not only inspires you to Play Big and Brand Bold but it gives you some of the lessons I've learnt along the way. It lets you know that you can choose where your life and business end up and that you have what it takes – we all do, actually – but it's how we use it that makes all the difference.

So, go forth and be amazing. Do big things. Build a confidently bold brand so you and your business aren't swimming in the sea of sameness, and keep Playing Big and Branding Bold!

I'll see you soon for my next book on building a standout personal brand – Amplify!

ABOUT THE AUTHOR AND SPEAKING OPPORTUNITIES

Suzanne Chadwick is the CEO & Founder of The Connection Exchange. A business, brand and speaker coach, she works with savvy women in business as well as training individuals in SMEs and corporate businesses. To find out more head to **www.suzchadwick.com** A regular conference speaker on building a standout business and personal brand, Suz Chadwick will teach your audience how to take their brand from basic biscuits to amazing 'got to have' goodness through an engaging, entertaining and dynamic session. You can contact her at **Suzanne@suzchadwick.com** to find out more or enquire about booking her for your next speaking event or for podcast interviews.

BRAND BUILDER'S ACADEMY

If you enjoyed this book and want to take your business and confidence to the next level then head over to **www.suzchadwick.com/bba**

Brand Builder's Academy is an eight-week online course to support savvy women who want more structure, strategies and systems to scale their business.

By the end of the program, you'll be able to:

- Develop a stronger mindset to play bigger in your business
- Build a brand strategy that positions you as the go-to person in your market
- Confidently show up and market yourself (even if you'd rather hide behind your computer)
- Design and implement systems that allow your business to scale (while taking the pressure off you)
- Create a strategic plan to build the business you want (even if your task list seems never-ending)
- Develop pricing and packaging that is clear and confident
- Build a rockstar brand experience for your clients

I created the Brand Builder's Academy to support you to uncover what's holding you back, equip you with the tools and resources to play a bigger game in your business, and create the success and abundance you've been dreaming of.

BRAND BUILDER'S LAB

The Brand Builder's Lab podcast can be found on all podcast apps. On this podcast we share solo episodes and interviews with business owners who are testing and trying new things out to build and grow their business and brand. Make sure you subscribe and catch a fresh episode every week!

www.suzchadwick.com/podcast

Let's Hang on
S O C I A L

—

You can find me on
all social platforms.

@SuzChadwick